Money Matters for

WORKBOOK

Age 15–18 Edition

Money Matters for

WORKBOOK
Age 15–18 Edition

Written by
Larry Burkett
with **Todd Temple**

Illustrated by **Chris Kielesinski**

MOODY PRESS
CHICAGO

© 1998 by LARRY BURKETT
Illustrations © 1998 by LAUREE AND L. ALLEN BURKETT

Project Coordinator: *L. Allen Burkett*
Editor: *Adeline Griffith*

For Lightwave
Project Editor: *K. Christie Bowler*
Art Director: *Terry Van Roon*
Illustrater: *Chris Kielesinski*
Inker: *Ken Save*

Adapted and rewritten from *Get a Grip on Your Money.*

Scripture taken from the New American Standard Bible, ©1960, 1962, 1963, 1968, 1971, 1972, 1973, 1975, 1977 by The Lockman Foundation. Used by permission.

ISBN: 0-8024-6346-0

6 7 8 9 10

Printed in the United States of America

Contents

Introduction

It's an unfortunate fact that we are sending our young people off into a very complicated world, unprepared to make the financial decisions they will be facing. Most young people today enter college thinking there is no alternative to borrowing and, yet, fully half of all student loans aren't spent on education. Instead, they are used to buy cars and stereos and even to take vacations. The struggles of repaying these loans will financially strap many young people for years after college.

Parents cannot abdicate the teaching of finances to the schools, because the schools aren't teaching it. It's astounding to think that you can get through elementary school, high school, and college and still not know how to balance a checkbook, or buy a home, or decide what kind of insurance you need. But, unfortunately, that's the norm.

Today, college students can borrow thousands of dollars for their education. In addition, they have credit cards, car loans, and automatic teller cards. As a result, they often start their working careers tens of thousands of dollars in debt. People don't intend to borrow so much money that they lose their cars, their homes, and even their families. They make these decisions out of a lack of understanding.

It's sad that half of all marriages today fail and, overwhelmingly, the major factor is the mismanagement of *money*. However, these statistics aren't inevitable. The problems can be avoided if the right decisions are made early enough—decisions like how to use credit cards wisely; how to live on a budget; and how to know what kind of cars, clothes, and houses to buy. *Money Matters for Teens Workbook Age 15–18 Edition* is definitely a step in the right direction.

The goal of this workbook is to give you, based on God's Word, the knowledge and resources to face the complex choices of our society. You also will find the companion book, *Money Matters for Teens,* helpful in learning God's principles of handling money. This book was produced by my son and daughter-in-law, Allen and Lauree Burkett. They've founded Money Matters for Teens™ and Money Matters for Kids™ to teach young people the principles of stewardship. Look for their logo (as it appears on this workbook) on other titles that were created with you in mind.

If we are ever going to develop a financially sound society, the best place to start is with our youth. If, as a teen, you are prepared to face the world of automated banking, free-wheeling credit cards, and easy government loans, you'll be well on your way to becoming the steward God wants you to be.

This study may be the best investment you'll ever make.

Larry Burkett

CHAPTER
1
Money Basics

Chapter 1

Money Basics

The average American teenager spends nearly $3,000 a year. Does that number seem too high to you? Add up all the money you get from your parents, plus any jobs. And don't forget those birthday checks. Your total may be less than $3,000, but it still adds up to a decent stack of cash. Let's look at where your money went—and why.

Learning About Money

Money is one of the world's most popular inventions. Just about everyone enjoys having money. We like to win money. We like to save money. And we *love* to spend money.

American teenagers spend over $90 *billion* each year! What's more, everyone from Nike to Nintendo knows this fact—and they want their share. The people who sell music, movies, munchies, make-up, milk shakes, and Macintoshes have your number. And they are running it through their calculators and thinking, "How much money can we get teenagers to spend on *our* products?"

If you don't take control of your money, someone else will.

Why should you learn how to manage your money? Because if *you* don't, *someone else* will. Youth marketers are spending billions in advertising, employing an army of marketing experts, and inventing powerful and creative ways to separate you from your money.

Of course, some of what they sell is stuff you need. And much of it is stuff that makes your life more enjoyable. But wouldn't you like to have *more* money to buy the things that are important to you and at the same time experience the following?

- Pay fair prices for quality items.
- Avoid being ripped off by misleading ads and salespeople.
- Stay out of debt.

- Save up for a car, college, your own business.
- Give money that will make a difference in the world.
- Have money to do fun things with your friends.

That's what this book is all about. We'll show you how to take back the control of your money so you can do these things. You'll learn skills that will help you right now *and* prepare you for a successful financial future. These skills work on *any* amount of money: a $5 allowance or a $5,000 paycheck. Whatever your financial situation, you can manage it with these skills.

Count Your Money

How much money passes through your hands in a year? In the spaces below, write how much money you get on average in a year. If you can't remember what you got last year, calculate it on one month and multiply by twelve. You'll be surprised!

Allowance: If you receive allowance weekly, multiply it by 52.   TOTAL _____

Odd jobs: If you have or had a variety of odd jobs, you might want to list them separately. For example, newspaper route, babysitting, mowing lawns.

1. _____   4. _____
2. _____   5. _____
3. _____   6. _____   TOTAL _____

Extra money from parents: This might include money you borrowed while you were out shopping (don't forget to repay it) or just extra gifts of money for specific needs, outings, and so on. We've suggested some categories and left blanks for others.

1. Lunch money: _____   4. Gift: _____
2. Outings: _____   5. _____
3. Achievement reward: _____   6. _____   TOTAL _____

Birthday: _____   _____   TOTAL _____

Christmas: _____   _____   TOTAL _____

Gifts from others besides your parents: aunts and uncles, family friends.

1. _____   3. _____
2. _____   4. _____   TOTAL _____

Other money you received from places other than those mentioned above.

1. _____   3. _____
2. _____   4. _____   TOTAL _____

Now add the totals from all the sections.   **YEAR TOTAL** _____

How To Buy Money

Before we talk about how to manage money, you need to understand where money comes from. As our parents have told us (3,000 times), "Money doesn't grow on trees."

Simply put, you actually *buy* money. Does that sound weird? You can purchase money with all sorts of things.

You can buy money with *stuff*. If you're a farmer, you pay in pigs, peaches, or potatoes. If you own real estate, you can offer acres, apartments, or office buildings. Just about *anything* can be used to purchase money—that is, if somebody wants what you have and has enough money.

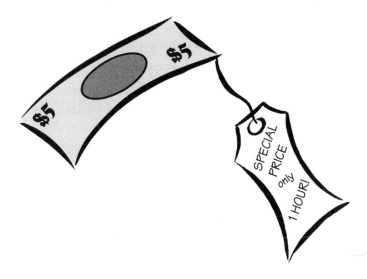

Most of us buy our money with our time and talents. Talents come in different denominations: You can buy $5 in one hour if you know how to alter someone's dress. You can buy $5,000 in an hour if you can replace someone's heart. The more talent you have, the more that hour is worth (as long as someone's willing to trade with you).

Of course, time doesn't grow on trees either. Every hour you sell for money is no longer available for other investments—friendships, family, God, education, fun, and sleep. How much time you sell depends on how much these other priorities are worth to you.

Putting a Price Tag on Money

Some people pay a very high price for money. They sacrifice their families, their friendships, their faith. In other words, they "pay the price" with these things. (So *that's* where the expression came from!)

Where your treasure is, there will your heart be also.
—Jesus

What's money worth to you? You set the price. You need a certain amount of money to support other priorities. (Your mom or dad sells time *away* from the family so he or she can afford to buy time *with* the family—a family that's fed and clothed and under a roof.)

If saving money for your future, or giving to your church, or helping the needy, or going on a trip with your youth group is important to you, you'll have to sell some time to do it. In a way, time *is* money.

Good money management gives you more money and more time for what's important to you.

That's why you must take control of your money. If you waste money through bad management, you have less money for your priorities. Then you have to spend more time *working* to buy more money—time away from your priorities.

All of this money management stuff is especially important for Christians. The Bible tells us that God is the owner of everything in this world. That includes you, your time, and your money. You don't really *own* anything! You're just managing these things for God.

God wants you to make wise investments with *His* time and money. He has great plans for you. He wants you to use this time and money to make a difference in the lives of the people around you. If you waste His resources, you can't do all the great things He's got planned for you. If you manage wisely, He'll use you to rock the world!

The lessons in this book will help you take the control of this time and money away from marketing and salespeople, lenders, and employers, and put it where it belongs: with you and God.

Rewind

1. American teenagers spend over $90 billion a year. Youth marketers know that—and they want their share.

2. Good money management takes the control of your money out of youth marketers' hands.

3. Most people get money by selling their time.

4. You set the price on money. What you're willing to pay for it depends on your priorities.

5. Good money management gives you more money and more time for what's important in your life.

CHAPTER
2
How Banks Work

ONE... ONE DOLLAR!
HA-HA-HA
TWO ... TWO DOLLARS!
HA-HA-HA

RYAN'S FIRST ACCOUNT

Chapter 2
How Banks Work

Nearly everyone in the country has some kind of bank account. Amazingly, most people don't know much about how banks work. You're about to learn what banks do with your money: where it goes, how they figure interest, and how they can help you save more money. By the end of this chapter, you'll know more about banking than most adults. Let's step into the vault.

The Money Store

You probably live pretty close to a grocery store. The grocer provides an important service in your community. He buys food products from farmers, dairies, food companies, and other *suppliers*; then, he sells these items to *customers*.

Your neighborhood bank does the same thing—except that they don't sell food; they sell *money*. The bank "buys" money from *suppliers*—you and everyone else with a savings account—and *pays* interest for the money. Then the bank "sells" the money to *customers*—businesses and individuals who take out loans—and *charges* interest for the money.

The grocer buys the products *wholesale* and sells it *retail*. The banker "buys" the money at *lower interest* and "sells" it at *higher interest*. Of course, you don't hear bankers talking about buying and selling. They call it borrowing and lending.

GROCERY STORE	LOCAL BANK
buys from suppliers at wholesale prices	*borrows* from depositors at lower interest rates
sells to customers at retail prices	*lends* to borrowers at higher interest rates

Bank Words

annual percentage rate:	(APR) the interest rate the bank pays over one year
balance:	the total principal and interest in your account
compound interest:	interest that's paid on the principal *and* any interest earned so far
interest:	fee banks pay depositors for the use of their money
principal:	any money *you* deposit in the account (as opposed to interest, which the *bank* pays into your account)
register:	paper form used to record your account activity: deposits, withdrawals, interest payments
simple interest:	interest that's paid on the principal only
statement:	computer-printed copy of bank's record on your account for one month
transaction:	any change made in your account, such as a deposit or withdrawal
yield:	the amount of interest your investment produces, figured as a percentage of the investment

Money Jugglers

Many people think that when they deposit money in a savings account, the bank simply stores the cash in the vault, where it gathers dust until they want it back. It doesn't work that way. Banks aren't money *warehouses*—they're money *stores*. They put that money to work by lending it to others and charging them interest on the loan.

Here's how it works. Let's say that you and nine of your friends have each scraped together $1,000. You all march down to the bank and invest your money in savings accounts paying 5 percent interest. The bank loves you! That's because the bank can now take each of your $1,000 deposits and lend a full $10,000 to someone else at 10 percent interest. They can afford to pay your interest (and everyone else's) and still make a profit.

But what happens on the day you and your friends decide to withdraw your $1,000 deposits? The bank can't ask the borrower to return all the money. They don't have to. On the day of your big withdrawal, the bank has plenty of cash because many other customers have made deposits. They also have a mailbox full of loan payments from borrowers. And, just in case, they also keep enough "spare change" in their vault to cover many withdrawals.

Banks are constantly juggling money. If they need more money to lend to people, they may offer a better interest rate on their savings accounts. This will attract more people to open accounts and deposit their money at the bank. Then the bank lends this new money to new borrowers and charges them enough in interest to cover the interest they're paying on their savings accounts.

Your Savings Account

Now that you've seen the big picture, let's look at the details. How do they take care of *your* savings account? When you deposit your money in a savings account, the bank pays you a fee for letting them use it. The fee is called *interest*. The interest is based on a percentage of your balance.

Simple Interest

Compound Interest

Let's say that the bank pays 12 percent interest on your savings account. (That's much higher than you're likely to get in a *real* bank, but let's use it for illustration.)

On official documents and advertisements, the bank will print "12 percent APR." The APR stands for Annual Percentage Rate, which is their way of saying that the interest is figured over a period of one year. If you deposit $100 in your account, you should receive $12 in interest at the end of one year, right? Wrong. Here's why.

There are basically two types of interest: *simple* interest and *compound* interest. Simple interest is figured only on the *principal*—your investment. In the example at left, the $100 is your principal. The $12 would be the simple interest you earn on your principal. It's that simple. But banks don't pay simple interest—and that's a good thing for you. (Banks often *charge* simple interest on loans. For more on simple interest, see Chapter 7, Anatomy of a Loan.)

Banks pay the second type of interest: *compound interest.* Here's the difference: At the end of the first month, the bank pays you the share of the interest you've earned on your principal *so far.* They can't pay you 12 percent; that's an *annual* rate. So they pay you one month's worth: *one–twelfth* of 12 percent. Of

First Month	
starting balance:	$100.00
monthly interest rate:	x .01
interest:	= $1.00
starting balance:	+ 100.00
new balance:	= $101.00

course, that's 1 percent. One percent of $100 is $1. Now you have $101 in your account: That's $100 in principal and $1 in interest.

At the end of the second month they do the same thing. They pay you one percent interest on the entire balance in your account—principal *and* interest. Here's the important part. Every month, the bank calculates the interest you've earned on the *entire* balance: principal and all the interest you've earned so far. In other words, the bank is paying interest on the interest. And that's what's called *compound interest*.

By the way, there's no rule that says a bank must compound the interest *monthly*. Some accounts pay interest *daily*. This means they divide the annual interest rate by 365 (instead of 12) and multiply that day's balance by this tiny interest rate. All those smaller interest payments add up to a better deal for you.

The Yield

We've gone ahead and calculated the monthly, compounding interest on the above deposit for the rest of the year. At the end of twelve months, the balance is $112.68. You've earned $12.68 in interest. But wait. If the bank *pays* 12 percent interest, why did you *receive* 12.68 percent?

Second Month	
starting balance:	$101.00
monthly interest rate:	x .01
	————
interest:	= $1.01
starting balance:	+ 101.00
	————
new balance:	= $102.01

That's the beauty of compound interest on a savings account. The interest *on the interest* adds up to more than the annual percentage rate. The 12.68 percent you actually received is called the *yield*. It's a word that farmers use to describe how much crop a particular acre of land produces in one season. In the money world, it's used to describe how much money a particular investment *produces* in one year.

When you're shopping around for a savings account to invest in, compare the yields (banks publish the yield next to the percentage rate). An account that yields 5.25 percent pays $5.25 in interest on a $100 investment for one year. A 6.5 percent yield pays $6.50 in interest on the same investment for the same period. It's pretty simple to compare that way.

A cash register keeps records of sales.

A check register keeps records of account activities.

Keeping Track

One of the purposes of this book is to show you how to manage money wisely. That means keeping track of your money: what you earn, spend, give, and save. Let's work on that last one for a bit: tracking what you save.

When you open a savings account, your bank may give you a *savings account register*. This little booklet contains columns and boxes that make it easy to record your deposits, withdrawals, and interest payments. We've reprinted a page from a savings account register that you can use to record some imaginary transactions.

Step 1: Make and Record Your Transactions

Let's say that you open a savings account on March 1 and deposit $50. A week later you deposit $10. The next week, $20. And during the last week of the month, you put in another $5. Each time you make a deposit, the bank gives you a receipt, called a *deposit slip*.

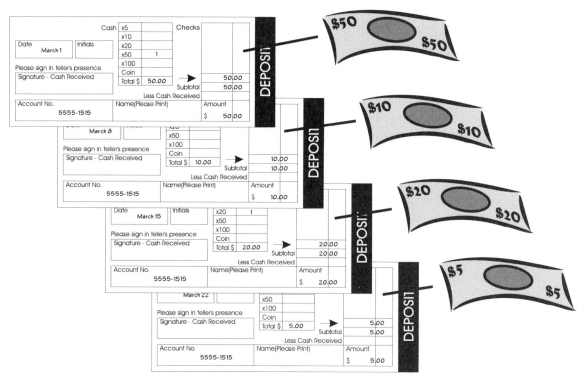

Now record these deposits in your register. We've done two of the deposits for you to show you how it's done. Notice how we used two lines for each deposit entry: This gives you room to add the deposit to the old balance in the right-hand column. For each entry, make sure you add the deposit to the old balance to get the new balance.

The last number in the right-hand column is your balance. You should have $85.00 in your account. (If you don't, check your addition.)

PERSONAL SAVINGS ACCOUNT RECORD				
DATE	TRANSACTION	DEPOSIT (+)	WITHDRAWAL (-)	BALANCE
				0.00
3/1	Opening Deposit	50.00		50.00
				50.00 ← Add old balance
3/8	Deposit	10.00		10.00 ← to deposit
				60.00 ← to get new balance

Step 2: Record the Interest

At the end of the month, your bank sends you a *statement*. This sheet of paper is a copy of *their* record of your account activity. It lists all deposits, withdrawals, and the interest that you've earned. Compare the bank's statement with your register to make sure that they've recorded all your transactions.

You need to make one more entry in your register: interest. As we showed earlier, calculating the interest on your account can get kind of complicated. The bank uses a computer to track your account activity and calculate the interest accordingly. It was the bank's computer that printed the statement. The statement shows that you've earned an incredible *25 cents* for the month! Okay, so it's not much, but it's a start. Treat the interest like a *deposit* and enter it in your register:

DATE	TRANSACTION	DEPOSIT (+)	WITHDRAWAL (-)	BALANCE
3/31	Interest	0.25		0.25
				$85.25

Now your register shows an account balance of $85.25. Pretty simple, isn't it? You'll be using this kind of account register in the next few chapters to track other accounts.

Changing Your Future

Many teenagers treat their savings account as a *spending* account. They store their money there for a few weeks or months, then take it out to spend it on something. This is a bad habit, and it only gets worse as they grow older.

Someday, you'll need a large chunk of money to buy a car or pay for college or start a business. But if you've been keeping a "spending account," most of your money will have been spent on shoes, CDs, clothes, fast food, sports toys, and a hundred other small and less-important things. Then your only choice is to *borrow* the money. So instead of *earning* interest from the bank on all that money, you're *paying* interest to the bank! It doesn't have to go this way.

Believe it or not, you can alter the course of your future—in a big way—*right now*. You can save yourself thousands of dollars. You can make it possible to afford the big stuff that you'll really need. And you'll spend the rest of your life thanking yourself for taking these steps. Are you ready to hear them? Here they are.

1. **Make a deposit in your savings account *every* week.**
2. **Don't make *any* withdrawals until you're ready to buy a car or go to college or make some other kind of major investment.**

You don't have to put *all* your money in the account! Just put *something* in your account every week—even a couple of bucks, if that's all you can afford. Just get into the consistent habit of setting aside some of your money. It may not seem like much; you won't get rich on the interest. But over time you'll accumulate enough money to

do something significant. And the interest you save on loans in your future (loans you won't need!) *will* make you rich!

In Chapter 5, Money Management Made Easy, we'll show you how to budget your money so you can have spending money *and* a growing savings account. But the first step is to start saving now, even if you don't have much.

Extra Extra

1. If you don't already have a savings account, open one this week.

2. Start a register of your account activity and keep it current by entering all transactions and interest payments.

3. Ask your bank for information on your account: the annual percentage rate, the yield, and how often they compound the interest (e.g., daily, monthly).

Open a Savings Account

After getting a feel for how an account works, go to your bank and open a savings account. Even better, open both a short-term savings *and* a long-term savings account.

Start a register for your banking account activity and keep track of all the money in and out.

Rewind

1. Banks are in the money business: they borrow the money from depositors at lower interest and lend it to borrowers at higher interest.

2. There are two types of interest: *simple interest* and *compound interest*.

3. Simple interest is paid only on the *principal* (your investment).

4. Banks pay compound interest, which is paid on the principal *and* any interest earned so far.

5. Use an account register to record all account activity: deposits, withdrawals, and interest payments.

6. Banks send monthly *statements* to show you their record of your account activity. Always compare your register with the statement to make sure everything is correct. Record your interest payment in the register—it's listed on your statement.

7. A savings account is for saving, not spending. Make regular deposits and keep your money in the bank until it's time to make a major investment.

notes

Money Matters for Teens

CHAPTER
3
Checking Accounts

Chapter 3

Checking Accounts

In this chapter you'll learn all about checking accounts—why they were invented, how they work, and how to write a check. Most important, you'll learn how to keep a running record of your checking account, so you'll always know how much money you have—or don't have. Checking accounts are simple to use and easy to understand. Read further.

Checks are really a great invention. Before checks were invented, people paid in cash. If you wanted to buy something but didn't have the cash on you, you had to ride your horse to the bank, get the money, and bring it back to the store to pay for your purchase.

Then someone came up with an idea: Write a permission note to the bank, give it to the person you're buying from, and have that person go to the bank for the cash. The note basically would give the bank permission to withdraw the stated amount from your account and give it to the person holding the note.

As you can imagine, writing permission notes all the time gave people writer's cramp, so someone came up with an even better idea: Print a stack of permission slips that already have your name and account number on them. All you have to do is fill in the name of the person getting the money, write the amount they're getting, and sign your name. These preprinted permission slips are called *checks*.

one…two…three…four

Why do people write out the numbers on checks ("four hundred"), rather than just use the numbers ($400)? There are two reasons.

1. An unscrupulous person might be tempted to add a zero to a handwritten "$400" and cash your check for $4,000. That's not so easy to do when you write out the numbers: you can't make "four hundred" look like "four thousand."

2. By writing the amount twice—once in numbers and once in letters—there's less confusion about the amount. Is that a 1 or a 7? Is that a decimal point or a comma? The written amount settles any confusion.

Things got even easier when banks started accepting each other's checks. Instead of hiking all the way across town to cash the check at your bank, the person with your check could take it to his or her own bank.

All banks have their own "checking account" at the Federal Reserve Bank. Here's how it works. Let's say you write a check for $20 to your friend Sarah. She cashes the check at her bank and gets $20 in cash. Sarah's bank sends your check to the Federal Reserve Bank. This "bank for banks" transfers the money from your bank's "bank account" to Sarah's bank. Then the Federal Reserve Bank sends the check back to your bank.

Now your bank is out $20, so it transfers that much money from your checking account and deposits it back into their Federal Reserve Bank account. Then your bank sends you the well-traveled, canceled check as proof that they had your permission to take the $20 out of your account (or that transaction shows on your monthly statement). Sound complicated? Not if you remember that the check is merely a permission note that's making its way back to your bank.

But a check is more than a permission note. It's a promise. When you write a check, you're promising the *payee* (the person you're giving the check to) that you have the cash in your bank account. If you don't, the bank will refuse to "honor" it (cash the check), and you've "bounced" the check. Instead of being converted to cash, it "bounces back" into the payee's hands—unpaid. The payee is left with a worthless piece of paper, and you've broken your promise.

Most checks bounce because people don't keep an accurate record of their checking accounts. They think they have enough money in their accounts to cover the checks they have written, but there is not enough to honor the promise. In the next chapter you'll learn more about how to prevent bouncing a check. But first, let's practice using a checking account.

Check Words

activity:	changes in the account balance, including deposits, withdrawals, checks cashed, service fees
bounced check:	a check the bank returns to payee unpaid because the account didn't contain enough money to cover it
NSF:	Not Sufficient Funds—the bank's polite way of saying the check bounced—not enough money in the account
payee:	the person or company you wrote the check to
register:	printed form used to record your transactions

Why People Use Checks

- safer to use than cash
- safer to mail
- more convenient than going to the bank every time you need to pay someone
- canceled checks provide a record of your spending

Step 1: Make a Deposit

Let's say that you've just opened a checking account at Great Bank. Your checkbook contains checks, deposit slips, and a check register for keeping track of your transactions. You have no money in the account yet, so let's make a deposit. You've picked up some money doing odd jobs around the neighborhood. One person paid you $80 in cash to take care of her pets while she was on vacation. Another neighbor gave you a check for $120 for painting his porch.

To deposit this money into your account, fill out a deposit slip taken from the back of your checkbook.

Today's Date

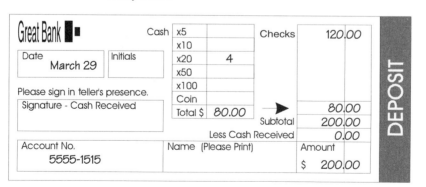

Great Bank	Cash	x5	
		x10	
Date March 29	Initials	x20	4
		x50	
Please sign in teller's presence.		x100	
Signature - Cash Received		Coin	
		Total $ 80.00	

Checks 120.00
Subtotal 200.00
Less Cash Received 0.00

Account No. 5555-1515

Name (Please Print)

Amount $ 200.00

DEPOSIT

Check ($120.00)

Cash ($80.00)

Subtotal (add the amounts)

Less Cash (0.00)

Total Deposit

Now turn to the *register* in the front of the checkbook and record the deposit.

		RECORD ALL CHARGES OR CREDITS THAT AFFECT YOUR ACCOUNT				
NUMBER	DATE	DESCRIPTION OF TRANSACTION	PAYMENT/ DEBIT (-)	DEPOSIT/ CREDIT (+)	BALANCE	
					0.00	
	03/29	Deposit - porch & pooch		200.00	200.00	
					200.00	

Write deposit amount here too.

Add the deposit to your previous balance ($0) to get the new balance.

Check no. (leave blank)

Today's Date

"Deposit - porch & pooch"

Amount of the deposit

Your check register is the most important part of your checkbook. Always write every transaction in it. Right now your register should show $200 as the last number in the right-hand column. That's your *balance*: you have $200 in your account. It's not enough to buy a new car, but it is enough to pay for some things you need to take care of right away. Let's write some checks.

Step 2: Write and Record Checks

You have three checks to write for this exercise. The first check goes to the Mission Fund—a $40 donation to help a friend go on a mission trip this summer. The second check goes to your dad, who lent you $50 last week, and you want to pay him back. The third check goes to The Great Big Boot Company—you're ordering a cool pair of boots.

Yes, I support our student missionaries on this special project.

☐ $10.00   ☐ $20.00   ☑ $40.00

Please make checks payable to "Mission Fund"

Pay back Dad $50.00

GREAT BIG BOOT COMPANY

ITEM	SIZE	PRICE/UNIT	NO. UNITS	PRICE
Great Big Boots	10	$70.00	1	$70.00

	SHIPPING & HANDLING	$5.00
	TOTAL	$75.00

Please make checks payable to "Great Big Boot Company."
(Allow 5 weeks for delivery)

Here are three checks pulled from your checking account and your check register showing your $200 balance. The first check has been written for you so you can see how it's done. (But be sure to sign and date the check!) Go ahead and write the next two checks. Be sure to record the information in your register, *subtracting* the check amount from your old balance to get your new balance.

Your Name
Your Address

001

Date (Today's Date)

Pay to the order of   Mission Fund $ 40.00

Forty ——————————————————————— 00/100 Dollars

Biff's Bank
Biffville, USA
Account #55555-1515

(Sign Here)

I: 1232958789 I: 123958   102

Your Name
Your Address

002

Date _____

Pay to the order of _____ $ _____

_____ Dollars

Biff's Bank
Biffville, USA
Account #55555-1515

I: 1232958789 I: 123958   102

Your Name
Your Address

003

Date _____

Pay to the order of _____ $ _____

_____ Dollars

Biff's Bank
Biffville, USA
Account #55555-1515

I: 1232958789 I: 123958   102

RECORD ALL CHARGES OR CREDITS THAT AFFECT YOUR ACCOUNT					
NUMBER	DATE	DESCRIPTION OF TRANSACTION	PAYMENT DEBIT (-)	DEPOSIT/ CREDIT (+)	BALANCE
					0.00
		Deposit - porch & pooch		200.00	200.00
					200.00
001		Mission Fund	40.00		-40.00
					160.00

Are all three checks completed, dated, and signed? Are all three recorded properly in your register? Is your running balance in the right-hand column complete? Your new balance should be $35. If it's not, go back and check your subtraction.

Keeping a checking account takes some work. You've got to record every deposit and every check and keep an accurate balance in that right-hand column. It takes a few moments to do it right. But it's not nearly as much work as writing individual permission notes to your bank or taking a trip to the bank each time you need to give money to someone.

Here's the best part: If you can keep accurate records in a register, you can handle just about any "accounting" task! Later on in the book, we'll show you how to track *all* your money—how much you earn, save, give, and spend. You can do it . . . if you know how to keep a check register.

Start "Checking"

Open your own checking account. If you want more practice in check writing, ask your parents if you can complete some checks for them.

1. Remember not to sign the checks; your name is not on the account so the bank would not accept it.

2. Fill in their check register with the check number, amounts, and payee (who the checks were for).

3. Subtract the check amount from the balance. Check your math.

4. When you feel you've got a handle on checking accounts, go to your bank and open a checking account of your own.

Extra Extra

Ask your parents if you can write some checks for them. Fill out the checks (but don't sign them!) and record everything in the check register.

Rewind

1. A check is a permission note: It gives your bank permission to take money from your account and give it to someone else.

2. A check is a promise: You're promising the payee that you have money in your account to cover the check.

3. A "bounced" check returns to the payee unpaid because the writer of the check doesn't have enough money in the account to "honor" the check.

4. Most people who bounce checks do so because they don't keep accurate records of their account.

5. The most important part of a checkbook is the register.

6. The most important step to writing a check is recording the information in the register.

7. If you can handle a register, you can learn to track *all* your money transactions.

Reconciling a Checking Account

Chapter 4

Reconciling a Checking Account

When you write a check, you're making a promise. In this chapter we show you how to keep your promise. Your bank sends you a record of your account each month. Since they're the ones holding your money, it's essential to make sure that their record matches your register. You'll learn how to reconcile these two documents to keep your account—and your reputation—healthy.

Reconcilable Differences

In the previous chapter you learned how to make a deposit, write checks, and record these transactions in your check register. There's one more critical step to managing a checking account: *reconciling*.

Reconciliation is an idea you're already familiar with. Let's say that you and a friend have a disagreement. Sooner or later (sooner is better!), you shake hands or hug and settle your differences. In other words, you've *reconciled*.

When you reconcile your *checking account*, you settle any disagreement between your checkbook register and the bank's records on your account. Like you, the bank keeps a record of all the activity in your account—deposits, withdrawals, checks cashed. And, lots of times, their records add up to something different than your records. To be sure your relationship with the bank stays strong, you have to reconcile any disagreement in each other's records. Why would there be a disagreement? There are three main reasons.

1. Errors. It's pretty easy to make a math error; maybe you subtracted wrong. Or you forgot to record a check and you think you have more money in your account than you do. Or maybe the bank made an error. They make mistakes too.

2. Charges. Your bank may charge you a fee for keeping a checking account, or they may charge you a few cents every time you write a check. And if you bounce a check, or order custom-designed checks, you'll be charged for these things too, and the money will be taken directly from your checking account.

3. The "Float." You may have written a check and recorded it in your register, but the *payee* may not have cashed it yet, or the bank hasn't recorded the transaction yet. It's "floating" somewhere in the system, and until it "lands" back in your account the bank's record shows more money in your account than what your register shows.

If, for any of these reasons, you *think* you have more money in your account than is actually there, you run the risk of bouncing a check. And that's *not* a good thing.

So how can you be sure that your register matches the bank's record? The bank makes it pretty easy for you. Every month, they send you a *statement*. Your checking account statement is a copy of the bank's record of your transactions. By comparing the statement with your check register, you can spot the differences and update your register to match. Here's how.

Account Shopping

Banks generally charge you fees for keeping a checking account. Some charge you a monthly fee, others charge you a few cents for every check you write; some banks charge for both. You can often avoid paying fees by keeping a minimum balance—$100 or more. Before you open a checking account, shop around for the best deal.

If you write few checks a month, a per-check charge may be cheaper than keeping a minimum balance. That's because most checking accounts don't pay you interest on your money, so you may be better off keeping that extra $100 in your savings account.

The Bank Makes a Statement

Let's say that last month you made that $200 deposit in your new account and wrote the three checks from the previous chapter. At the end of the month you made one more deposit for $45. Here's a copy of your check register.

		RECORD ALL CHARGES OR CREDITS THAT AFFECT YOUR ACCOUNT				
NUMBER	DATE	DESCRIPTION OF TRANSACTION	PAYMENT DEBIT (-)	FEE (IF ANY) (-)	DEPOSIT/ CREDIT (+)	BALANCE
						0.00
		Deposit - porch & pooch			200.00	200.00
						200.00
001		Mission Fund	40.00			-40.00
						160.00
002		Dad	50.00			-50.00
						110.00
003		Great Big Boot Co.	75.00			-75.00
						35.00
		Deposit - yardwork			45.00	45.00
						80.00

At the end of the month, the bank mailed you a statement. It lists the deposits, the checks cashed, and any other charges. It looks something like this.

Checking Account Statement

Account Number: 5555-1515

CHECKS

date	check no.	amount
03/07	001	$40.00
03/10	003*	$75.00
3/15	004	$12.00

OTHER ACTIVITY

date	transaction	amount
03/01	DEPOSIT	$200.00+
03/05	CUSTOM CHECKS	$10.00-
03/31	SERVICE CHARGE	$5.00-

BALANCES

	OPENING BALANCE	$200.00
	CLOSING BALANCE	$58.00

As you can see, they don't match. For one thing, the closing balance on the statement is $58, but your register shows that you should have $80 in your account! Not to worry! Just reconcile your account to find out what happened. There are five steps.

Step 1: Compare Checks

Determine which checks have been cashed. Do this by placing a mark in the checkbook register next to each check number that's listed on the statement. Mark these check numbers on the statement too. In the above example, go ahead and put a check mark next to check numbers 001 and 003, because they're listed on both records.

Step 2: Compare Deposits and Withdrawals

Now do the same thing with deposits and withdrawals, marking each transaction that's listed on both your register and the bank statement. Remember to mark them in both places. In the above example, the initial deposit is listed in both places. Place a check mark next to your deposit on both records.

Step 3: Record Their Surprises

Look on their statement for unmarked transactions. If you find one, it means that you don't have a record of that transaction in your register. Maybe you forgot to record a check or an ATM withdrawal or you were charged a service fee. Record each of these missing transactions into your register and mark them off in both places as you do.

If you completed steps 2 and 3 correctly, you'll notice that there's no mark next to check number 004 on the statement. Where did this check come from? We forgot to tell you that you wrote a $12 check to your friend Luis for helping you paint that porch. Maybe that's why you forgot to record the check in your register. Well, go ahead and write the check in your register now; then mark the transaction in both places.

You'll also notice two other unmarked transactions on your statement: a $10 check-printing fee and a $5 service charge. Record each of these transactions in your register and mark them off in both places.

With these three new entries in your register, you now show a balance of $53 at the bottom of the right-hand column. The statement still says you have $58 in the account. Time to move to the next step.

Step 4: Add Your New Credits

All of *their* transactions are now in your register, but you may have a few transactions that didn't make it into their record before the statement was printed. First of all, look through your register for unmarked *deposits*. If you find any without a mark, flip the statement over and write down the amount of these "credits" on the worksheet you find there. Banks print this little worksheet to help you reconcile your account each month. Add the total of these credits to the bank's version of your balance.

We've printed a copy of this worksheet for you to fill out. The first line is where you write the statement balance as shown on the front side. Then there are some lines for writing down unmarked deposits. They must have printed your statement before you made that $45 deposit. Write that deposit on the worksheet and add it to the bank's version of your balance: $103. Now it's *really* off! Don't worry! Just move to the next step.

Step 5: Subtract Your New Debits

You may have some checks or ATM withdrawals that didn't get cashed or recorded in time to make it onto the bank statement. These "debits" are the ones listed in your register that don't have marks next to them. Write down these debit amounts on your worksheet and subtract them from the subtotal you got in step 4.

In the above example, there's one check listed in your register that's not on the bank statement: check number 002—the $50 check to your dad. He was so excited about being paid back that he put the check in a pocket and forgot about it. When he remembers, he'll take the check to the bank to cash it, so you had better account for it on the statement worksheet. Enter the $50 on the above worksheet and subtract it from the $103 subtotal. The "revised" statement now shows a balance of $53—same as your register. You're reconciled!

Maybe this reconciliation business seems complicated to you. The numbers can seem confusing, but the process is really simple. Basically, you're comparing two objects. When you check off all the things that the objects have in common, you can concentrate on the things that are different. Add the missing things to each object until they're identical.

What happens if you do all five steps and your number is still different than theirs? Someone made a mistake. Review the steps and make sure all transactions were recorded and marked properly. Then go over your calculations to be sure you didn't slip a digit somewhere. If you're sure that your numbers are right, then the error may be the bank's. They make mistakes too, and you may spot it while you're checking the figures. Go into the bank and show them the statement and your register. They'll fix the error.

Beware the Bouncing Check

Why is it necessary to go through all this trouble every month? If you don't know exactly how much money you have in your checking account, it's too easy to bounce a check. A bounced check is an expensive mistake: The bank charges you a "returned-check" fee and the payee of the check may charge you another fee. And if you wrote the check to a business, they may refuse to accept your checks in the future. Even worse, you've broken a promise.

As we mentioned earlier, people bounce checks when they fail to record all transactions in their check registers or fail to reconcile their accounts each month. If you do these two things, bouncing checks won't be a problem.

By the way, *if you master the art of keeping an accurate check register and reconciling your account, you're way ahead of most adults*! What's more, you can master just about any other money management skill. We'll prove it to you in later chapters.

Transactions

Credit: any deposit or transfer that puts money into your account

Debit: any check, ATM withdrawal, service fee or transfer that takes money out of your account

Account Shopping

Banks generally charge you fees for keeping a checking account. Some charge you a monthly fee, others charge you a few cents for every check you write; some banks charge for both. Often you can avoid paying fees by keeping a minimum balance—$100 or more. Before you open a checking account, shop around for the best deal.

If you write few checks a month, a per-check charge may be cheaper than keeping a minimum balance. That's because most checking accounts don't pay you interest on your money, so you may be better off keeping that extra $100 in your savings account.

How NOT to Bounce a Check

Bouncing checks is expensive and damaging to your reputation. Follow these tips to help you avoid writing bad checks.

- Record every transaction in your register as soon as you make it.

- Reconcile your statements as soon as they arrive.

- If you can't get your account to balance, go to your bank and ask for help.

- Set your own "minimum balance" and don't allow yourself to let the account dip below that amount. This will give you a margin for error.

Extra Extra

Ask a parent if you can reconcile the family checkbook. (Be careful—if you do a good job, this may become a permanent responsibility!)

Reconcile

When the first bank statement for your account comes, reconcile it with your checking account register. Go through all the steps outlined in this chapter. If you have any problems reconciling the two, ask your parents for help or go to the bank and ask a youth financial advisor (that's what they're there for).

Reconciliation Worksheet
Account Number: 5555-1515

Statement Balance from other side of statement:	$58.00	

Credits not listed on statement: _____   Enter $45.00
_____   deposit here.
_____
_____   Add credits to
Subtotal (statement balance + new credits): _____   statement balance

Debts not listed in statement: _____   Enter missing
_____   check amount here
_____
_____

Revised balance (subtotal - new debts) _____   Subtract debts
from subtotal

Rewind

1. The first step to reconciling your account is to compare the check record in your register with the bank's statement.

2. The second step is to compare other deposits and withdrawals on both records.

3. The third step is to enter missing transactions into your register.

4. The fourth step is to add your missing credits to the statement's worksheet.

5. The fifth step is to subtract your missing debits from the statement's worksheet.

6. Bouncing a check can be expensive—and damaging to your reputation.

7. You can avoid bouncing checks by recording all transactions in the check register and reconciling the account with the monthly statement.

Money Management Made Easy

Chapter 5

Money Management Made Easy

So far you've learned how to manage a savings account and a checking account. You now have all the skills you need to manage your money! We're about to take these skills and show you how to set up and maintain a budget, keep track of all your earning, saving, giving, and spending. . . and even how to have fun doing it. Let's get started.

You're about to learn something that 90 percent of all adults haven't figured out: How to control your money! You may not have a regular job, drawing a regular salary, but it is likely that at least *some* money passes into and out of your pocket or purse every week. We're going to show you how to take charge of that process. To help you get started, there's an easy formula:

AI minus T&T equals NSI

If you can remember that, you'll never have a problem with handling money— either now or in the future. It doesn't matter whether you make $10 a week or $15 million a year, it all works the same. Here's what it means.

AI stands for "Available Income." That's pretty self-explanatory, isn't it?

T&T in the formula means "Tithe and Taxes."

NSI means "Net Spendable Income." NSI is what you can *spend*.

It's simple: AI minus T&T equals NSI. Now let's put it to use.

AI = Available Income

Let's say that you take in about $50 each week from a job and allowance and whatever else you do for money. Whether you make more or less doesn't matter. We'll use $50 a week for this exercise to show you how simple it is to control your money. It's kind of obvious, but we'll say it anyway: Your average weekly Available Income is $50, so you can save and give and spend as much as you want—as long as you don't exceed that $50 AI.

T&T = Tithe & Taxes

Let's also say that you want to *tithe* money to your church, which means giving away a percentage of your income. We'll talk more about that in chapter 10, "How to Give Money Wisely." For now, let's say that you want to give 10 percent of your income to your church. That means $5 per week.

AI	$50
T&T	- $5
NSI	= $45

If you're making about $50 a week, you don't have to worry about taxes. In the U.S. you can make up to $4,000 per year without having to file a tax return. There are a couple of exceptions: If teenagers have any interest or dividend or capital gain income of $1 or more and earn from all income sources (earned and unearned) a total over $650 or more, they will have to file income tax returns. Also, if teenagers are self-employed, such as mowing yards or babysitting, they will have to file a return if their net income is $400.00 or more, because they will need to pay self-employment taxes (Social Security/Medicare). So, for now, let's not worry about taxes. (Enjoy that while you can.) One thing you might do is put aside 10 percent as a "family tax" that goes into a fund for family activities or purchases that everyone agrees to contribute to.

NSI = Net Spendable Income

Your NSI is what's left of your income after you set aside your tithe and taxes. In this example, that's $50 minus $10, or $40 per week in Net Spendable Income.

To build a proper budget, we need to divide the NSI into categories. We'll keep it simple for now. Let's say that you're saving for a car by depositing 40 percent of your income into a long-term savings account. Forty percent of $50 is $20. And you spend the rest of your NSI on food, entertainment or whatever. Here's what your budget looks like.

WEEKLY BUDGET

AI	$50
T&T	-$10
NSI	$40
Saving	- $20
Spending	- $20
	= $ 0

What could be simpler? If you can consistently manage to spend no more than your NSI, you're a wise money manager—no matter how much money you make. The only differences between this budget and that of a millionaire are the amount of money in each category and the number of categories in the budget. Later, we'll increase your income (yes!) and add some expense categories (sorry), but for now let's just work with what we've got.

The Envelopes, Please

The key to good money management is in controlling your NSI. We have a simple management system: Take four envelopes and label them. One is for your tithe: we'll call it "Giving." One is for "Taxes." The other two envelopes are for your NSI categories, "Long-Term Saving" and "Spending." These are the names of the four *accounts* in your system.

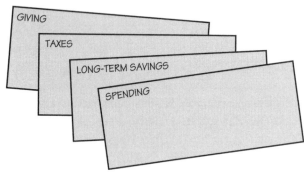

Of course, you can't have an account without an account *register*, so let's create four registers—one for each of these envelope accounts. Now it's time to *deposit* the money into the accounts. Take the $50 you earned this week and divide it among the envelopes: $5 in the GIVING envelope, $5 in the TAXES envelope, $20 in the LONG-TERM SAVINGS envelope, and $20 in the SPENDING envelope.

GIVING ACCOUNT - *for week of : April 1 - 7*

Date	Transaction	Deposit	Withdrawal	Balance
4/1	Deposit	5.00		5.00
				5.00

TAXES ACCOUNT - *for week of : April 1 - 7*

Date	Transaction	Deposit	Withdrawal	Balance
4/1	Deposit	5.00		5.00
				5.00

LONG-TERM SAVINGS ACCOUNT - *for week of : April 1 - 7*

Date	Transaction	Deposit	Withdrawal	Balance

SPENDING ACCOUNT - *for week of : April 1 - 7*

Date	Transaction	Deposit	Withdrawal	Balance

As you learned earlier, *every* account transaction must be recorded in the account's register. Here are the registers for these accounts. We've recorded the GIVING deposit to show you how it's done. Go ahead and record the correct LONG-TERM SAVINGS and SPENDING deposits in their respective registers.

Now that the money is in the account envelopes and you've recorded your deposits, it's time to take the money *out*. Let's say that on April 2, you take the money from the GIVING account envelope and drop it in the offering at church. Now record the transaction in the GIVING register as a *withdrawal*. Your balance in that account should now be $0.

Do the same with your TAXES. Take them from your envelope and deposit that money into whatever your family keeps the family "taxes" in. Record the transaction in your TAX register as a withdrawal. The balance is also $0.

The LONG-TERM SAVINGS account is even easier. Just deposit the envelope's contents into your *real* long-term savings account. This account register is your *actual* bank account register. It's not a withdrawal until you take the money out of your real savings account (which is something you're not going to do for a long time because you read Chapter 2 carefully).

This leaves us with the SPENDING account. Every time you spend money, you write down what you spent as a withdrawal. For this example, we've gone ahead and spent some money *for* you! Here's what was spent and for what. Go ahead and record each of these items as a withdrawal in your SPENDING account register.

4/2	fast food	$2.00
4/4	magazine	$5.00
4/5	more fast food	$3.00

If you subtracted correctly, you should have a balance of $10 in the right-hand column. What will you do with that extra cash? Leave it in the envelope! Next week, if you make less money, you'll still have this extra spending cash from this week.

If you would like to try this system for real, go ahead. Use your real savings account register for LONG-TERM SAVINGS, and create other accounts according to your own needs. We've printed a standard account register in the back of the book, which you can photocopy and label with your own account titles. You're on your own for the envelopes.

Budget Tricks

As you've probably guessed by now, if you want to make any large purchases, you're going to have to spend *less than* $20 each week and carry the balance from week to week. Here's a simple way to do it: Open a new account! Call it your SHORT-TERM SAVINGS account.

If you need to save $100 for a ski trip, adjust your budget accordingly, and deposit money into an envelope marked SHORT-TERM SAVINGS: SKI TRIP. If you set aside $6 a week, you'll make your goal in 17 weeks.

If you're like most teenagers, your income varies from week to week. Not a problem. In the above example, your first priorities—giving, taxes, and saving—are based on percentages. If you're committed to giving 10 percent, just divide *whatever*

you make by 10 and that's how much you give that week. If you're committed to putting 40 percent of your income in your savings account, multiply your earnings by .40 and deposit that amount.

Maybe some weeks you make so little that there's hardly anything to spend. Welcome to the real world. This is where budget planning pays off. Smart money managers set aside money in a "Just in Case" account. (Get out another envelope!) When they come into a dry week (no money), they reach into this special account to make ends meet. If you can't count on a regular income, spend a bit less on the good weeks and keep it there until you need it.

Here's another way to smooth out the bumps of a rocky income: Make longer-term budgets. Most adults get paid just once or twice a month, so they make monthly budgets. Some people, such as real-estate brokers, commissioned salespeople, and the self-employed, often go without regular paychecks. These folks make *annual* budgets because they know the money in their accounts must last for months. If your income is infrequent, make a monthly budget and then divide up the account balances to tell you how much you can afford each week.

A Budget That Works

If you have any kind of income, you can make a budget that works if you follow these steps.

1. Write your Available Income (AI).

2. Subtract your Tithe and Taxes (T&T).

3. Disburse your Net Spendable Income (NSI) among your other priorities and enter these amounts as deposits on individual account sheets.

4. Whenever you take money from an account, enter the transaction as a withdrawal from that account.

Your accounts may be different from our example. Your income is sure to be different. But the *system* is the same regardless of your income and priorities. Try the system for a few weeks. We're confident that it will help you save, give more money than before, and keep your spending under control. See for yourself.

NEW WEEKLY BUDGET	
AI	+ $50
T&T	- $10
NSI	= $40
Saving	- $20
Spending	- $ 6
Spending	- $ 9
Balance	= $ 5

Set Up a Budget

1. Calculate your average weekly income (or bi-weekly). $ _____

2. Divide it between the budget categories:

   Tithes/giving $ _____

   Long-term savings $ _____

   Short-term savings goal $ _____

   Spending $ _____

3. Write out this budget and get an envelope and account register for each priority on your budget list.

4. Begin putting your real money in your new budget!

   a. Deposit your long-term savings in your real account.

   b. Start a short-term savings account and deposit that money.

   c. Pay your tithe.

5. Record all your transactions in your account registers.

Rewind

1. The key budget formula is: AI - T&T = NSI (Available Income *minus* Tithe and Taxes *equals* Net Spendable Income).

2. A budget is your plan for managing your AI, however great or small.

3. Each category in your budget is a priority and has its own *account*. You disburse your income among these accounts.

4. Each account has its own *account register*: record your deposits and withdrawals in the register.

5. Carry any account balance into the next week.

6. When your priorities change, rework your budget and open new accounts.

CHAPTER 6

Controlling Bigger Budgets

Chapter 6

Controlling Bigger Budgets

We used a simple budget in the last chapter to show you how easy it is to keep track of your money. But what happens when you have a bigger income and dozens of monthly living expenses? This chapter will show you how the same budget and accounting system works for an adult—and how to customize it for yourself.

In the previous chapter, we used envelopes to separate the money physically into different accounts. It's easier to understand budgets and accounting that way. Well, now that you know how to do all the fancy accounting, it's time to tell you the truth: Most people don't keep their money in envelopes. (Okay, so you already knew that.) Here's how they do it.

Let's imagine that you have a checking account. When you receive your $50 in AI, you deposit *all* of it into this single account. (And record the transaction in your check register, of course!) Here's the cool part: All that money is *physically* in one account, but in your *budget*, it's divided into different accounts.

When you make that $50 deposit into your checking account, you also record the deposit in each of the Individual Account Sheets.

When you write checks, you record the transaction in the checking account register, as always. But you also record the transactions in the individual account registers. The tithe check is recorded as a withdrawal in the GIVING account. Any spending cash you take out of the checking account goes down as a withdrawal from the SPENDING account.

For the SAVINGS account, you *could* write a check to yourself and deposit it in your real savings account. But it's easier to have your bank savings account's actual register track that account and transfer the money between the bank accounts.

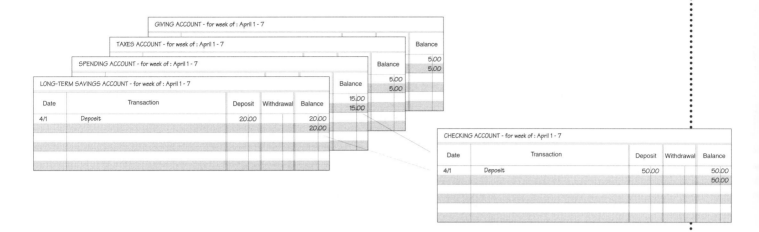

This seems like a lot of work! Why do it? Let's learn from the people who *don't* keep separate account registers. They put all their money in the checking account. When they need to pay for something, they look at their check register. If there's money in it, they figure they can afford it. But they forget that they're trying to set aside money for the church, or for that ski trip, or rent, or food! When the bills come, their account is empty. They're stuck.

By keeping separate account registers, you know exactly how much of the money in your checking account is available for each priority in your life. When it comes time to buy the things you need, the money you earned will be there.

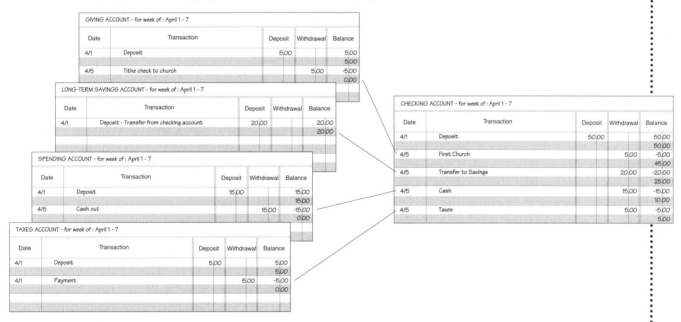

Right now you probably don't have a lot of expenditures, and you won't go without food or clothes or a place to live if you happen to mess up on your budget. But in a few years, your money management skills will keep food in the refrigerator, clothes on your back, and a roof over your head. *If you can manage a budget now, the future will be much brighter.*

An Adult Budget

As you get older, you can use this same budget system. Just open new accounts as you need them: Taxes (sorry), Housing, Food, Clothing, Auto (Transportation), Insurance, Entertainment/Recreation (yes!)—whatever you need to stay ahead of your money.

Most people are paid once or twice a month instead of weekly, so they set up *monthly* budgets. Let's look at one adult's budget to see how it's done.

Carlos is 22, fresh out of college, and living on his own in an apartment. He works as a graphic artist for a publishing company and makes $24,000 a year. His monthly *gross* income is $2,000, but his *take-home* pay, or AI, is only $1,500. That's because his company takes out about 25 percent of his earnings for income taxes, Social Security, medical insurance, and other deductions. Carlos has worked up a great budget that makes a lot of sense when you understand his priorities.

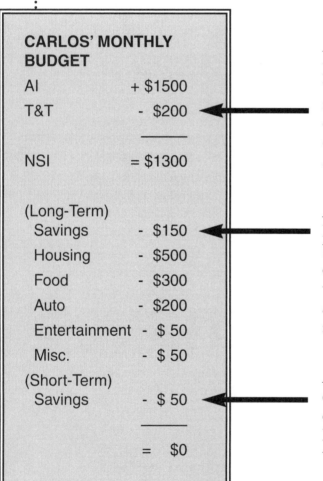

CARLOS' MONTHLY BUDGET

AI	+ $1500
T&T	- $200
NSI	= $1300
(Long-Term)	
Savings	- $150
Housing	- $500
Food	- $300
Auto	- $200
Entertainment	- $ 50
Misc.	- $ 50
(Short-Term)	
Savings	- $ 50
	= $0

Priority 1: Carlos is committed to tithing 10 percent of his *gross* income. Although he only takes home $1,500 each month, he *earns* $2,000, so he tithes on the full amount. And since his employer pays his taxes straight out of his earnings, he doesn't have to worry about setting aside additional tax money in his T&T category.

Priority 2: Carlos puts 10 percent of his NSI into a long-term savings account each month so he can buy his own home someday. His regular deposits don't amount to much now (when compared to the cost of a house!), but he knows that they all add up and, as his income grows, his percentage saving will really pay off.

Priority 3: Carlos is committed to staying out of debt. He disburses the rest of his NSI among the other expenses in his life. And he keeps a record of his transactions to be sure he's not spending more than he can afford.

Future Budget

Ask your parents to go over their monthly budget with you so you can see how an actual one works. Get them to explain why they allocate the amounts they do to each item.

Ask your parents if you can run the family finances for a month to learn to budget.

At the end of the month, with a parent's help, do a mock budget that outlines what you will need when you move out on your own or with a friend.

1. Use the budget form at the back of the book.

2. Decide if you will get a place alone or have roommates.

3. How much money will it take you to live? You will need basically the same categories your parents' budget has (e.g., Tithes, Savings, Housing, Food, Auto (includes bus fare or car payments and gas).

4. What is the total of your mock monthly budget?

5. That's how much money you will need to make ends meet each month. The next question: What kind of job will pay that? It's something to think about.

Cash Flow

Carlos deposits his paychecks in his checking account. He keeps a separate account *register* for each of his budget categories—Housing, Food, Auto. If he got one big $1,500 paycheck each month, his money management would be easy. He could deposit the paycheck and then pay his rent, utilities, and all of his other regular expenses right away.

But like most of us, Carlos doesn't get paid that way. Instead, he gets *two* paychecks: $750 on the first day of the month and another $750 on the 15th day of the month. Without separate account registers, he would have no way of knowing how much of each paycheck must be set aside for each account. Let's take a closer look at some of his accounts to see why this is important.

Housing: His rent ($400) is due on the first of every month. So he knows that most of his first paycheck must be set aside for rent. His utilities (phone, electric, and water bills—about $100) are due at the end of the month, so he pays these out of the second paycheck (on the 15th). During the summer months he spends less on utilities, so his Housing account balance grows a little during the warmer months. He doesn't spend the money on other things because he knows that the winter months are around the corner, and his heating bills will eat up the extra dollars left over from the summer.

Food: A quick look at his food account tells him he can spend $10 a day on food. If he spends $8 for lunch, it leaves only $2 for the rest of the day. So he takes his lunch to work on most days and treats himself to a restaurant meal once or twice a week. And if he splurges on a lobster dinner one night, he'll be eating rice and beans the rest of the week!

Auto: Carlos bought a good used car for cash a couple of years ago with the money he saved as a teenager, so he has no monthly loan payments. But he has to pay for insurance out of the second paycheck; gas money comes out of both paychecks. Some months he has as much as $50 left in the Auto account after the bills are paid, but the balance gets eaten up eventually with a repair bill or a tune-up charge.

	First Paycheck	Second Paycheck
AI	+ $750	+ $750
T&T	+ $100	+ $100
	———	———
NSI	= **$650**	= **$650**
(Long-Term)		
Savings	- $0	- $150
Housing	- $400	- $100
Food	- $150	- $150
Auto	- $50	- $150
Entertainment	- $25	- $25
Misc.	- $25	- $25
(Short-Term)		
Savings	-	- $50
	=====	=====
	= $0	= $0

Miscellaneous: This is where Carlos deducts money for things like a new reading lamp, haircuts, cleaning bill, CDs, vacation money—whatever isn't covered in his other accounts. He doesn't know exactly what he's going to be needing this money for, but there's always some expense that comes along that can't be covered in the other accounts. If he didn't have this account, he'd be tempted to take the money from his *savings*. But that would mess up his priorities. The Miscellaneous account helps Carlos to keep his budget and his priorities straight.

Short-Term savings: This is money saved for items that take a few weeks or months to save for—microwave oven, vacation, or mountain bike.

To make sure he has enough money to cover the big expenses, Carlos has divided his monthly budget into *two* budgets—one for each paycheck. Every paycheck goes into his checking account, but the amount allocated to each individual budget account varies according to which paycheck it comes from.

As Carlos's income grows (he's up for a raise soon) and his priorities and living expenses change, he can adjust his budget and create new accounts.

Personal Accountant

Now that you're a virtual *expert* in accounting, we want to clarify a couple of things that can cause confusion.

Register or Ledger? Throughout the book we've referred to the piece of paper used for recording an account's activity as a *register*. That's what most people call that little record booklet in their checkbook. When they keep their records on a sheet of paper, they often call it an account *ledger* or account *sheet*. They may not even use paper at all: Popular personal accounting programs such as *Money Matters* (from CFC) or *Quicken* allow them to track all their accounts on computer. What you *call* your account records isn't important. What's important is keeping accurate records of all accounts.

One Line or Two? Some people use *two* lines in their register/ledger/account sheet for each entry. That's what we've been doing in this book. Others use just *one* line for each entry, doing the math in their head or on a piece of scrap paper. The first method gives more room to write notes and do the math. The second method uses less room and looks neater. Choose the method that works best. The *correct* method is the one that keeps accurate records.

As you can see, there's a lot of flexibility in this accounting system. You can have three accounts or thirty accounts. You can store your money in a checkbook, envelopes, or a sock in the back of your drawer. You can call your account records *registers, ledgers,* or *account sheets.* You can use a one-line entry or a two-line entry.

The important part is that you make a budget, divide your money among the separate accounts, and record every deposit and withdrawal. If you can do these things, you can manage *any* amount of money: $10 or $10 *million.*

Rewind

1. You don't need to keep separate account *envelopes;* you do need to keep separate account *registers.*

2. Bigger expenses, such as rent or payment on a car or other vehicle, must be carefully considered in your budget. You must ensure that the account has enough money in it at the right time of the month.

3. To stock up an account to cover a bigger bill, deposit a larger portion of certain paychecks into the account. For example, deposit enough money from the first paycheck of the month to cover your rent. Use the second paycheck to cover other priorities.

4. A "miscellaneous" account can be used to cover unplanned and emergency expenses.

5. Some people call their account registers *ledgers* or *account sheets.*

6. Some people use two lines to enter transactions on their registers; others use one line. Use what works for you.

notes

_____

_____

_____

_____

_____

_____

_____

CHAPTER 7

Anatomy of a Loan

MY UNCLE PHIL HAD SO MANY LOANS, HE CONSOLIDATED THEM. THEN HE GOT A LOAN TO CONSOLIDATE HIS CONSOLIDATIONS. WHEN HE WAS WORKING ON A LOAN TO CONSOLIDATE HIS CONSOLIDATION OF HIS CONSOLIDATION LOANS, IT GOT SO CONFUSING, THE BANK HAD TO **HIRE** HIM TO HANDLE HIS OWN ACCOUNTS!

WHAT A GREAT WAY TO GET A JOB!

Chapter 7

Anatomy of a Loan

Loans are tricky things. Lenders use their own vocabulary and some pretty fancy math. We'll teach you some words, show you their calculations, and help you understand the wild world of borrowing.

Money for Rent

Let's say that some friends invite you to go snowboarding for the weekend. Problem: You have no board or boots, and buying new gear will cost you $500. Do you say no and stay at home that weekend? Probably not. That's because you found a store that will *rent* you the board and boots for just $30.

When you rent that snowboard, you don't own it. What you're "buying" is the *right to use* the thing for a limited time—the weekend. The owner of that equipment—the ski shop—sells you that right by charging you a rental fee. Nowadays you can rent just about anything: movies, mansions, moving vans, Mazda Miatas. You can even rent *money* (but be very careful about that and be sure to read Chapter 9 carefully).

Money rental works a lot like other rentals—only with different words: The owner of the money (the *lender* or *creditor*) sells you (the *borrower*) the right to use money for a limited time (the *term*). The rental fee is called *interest*.

Lenders are in the money-rental business.

People in the money-rental business calculate their fee on a percentage of the *principal*—the amount of money you rent. Let's say you borrow $100 for one year at 12 percent interest. At the end of the year, you return the $100, plus $12 in interest. Easy, right?

Not exactly. This is where there's a big difference between renting money and renting anything else.

When you rented the snowboarding equipment, you got to use all the gear for the entire weekend. You didn't have to give back the boots on Saturday and the board on Sunday. But money lenders generally expect you to give back a portion of the loan

Loan Words

amortized loan:	an installment loan that's paid off in multiple equal payments
APR:	annual percentage rate
balance:	in a credit card account, the total of all unpaid principal and interest
compound interest:	interest charged on principal and interest
finance charge:	the fees lenders charge for the use of their money, including interest, application fees.
installment loan:	a loan that's paid back in several payments, or installments, rather than all at once
interest:	the fee lenders charge for the use of their money—also called finance charge
minimum payment:	the least amount of money the creditor expects you to pay; generally enough to cover the interest, with not much left over to pay down the principal
period:	the fraction of a term used for computing interest and payments—generally one month
principal:	the amount of money you owe
revolving credit:	an open-ended loan arrangement, such as a credit card, that allows you to borrow and repay money gradually, rather than all at once.
term:	the length of a loan

each month. They call these monthly payments *installments* and refer to this type of loan as an *installment loan.*

Installment loans are easier for most people to handle. You don't get stuck with one giant payment at the end of the loan. Instead, you pay it back one portion at a time. An installment loan is also cheaper because you pay interest only on what you still owe, not on the full amount.

You may recall that your bank divides your savings account's annual interest by 12 and pays you *monthly* interest on the balance that month. The lender of an installment loan does the same thing—in reverse.

The $100 loan at 12 percent is paid off in 12 monthly installments. The monthly interest for the first month is easy to figure: one percent of $100 is $1.00. You send the lender the $1.00, plus a small part of the balance.

The next month you pay 1 percent interest on your balance, which is now less than $100 because you already paid some of it back. Each month you pay back a portion of the principal and pay 1 percent interest on what's left. At the end of the year, you've paid back the $100 plus $6.63 in interest.

Amazing Loans

1. To get the idea of what it costs to borrow money try this exercise. Let's pretend you have just borrowed $100,000 at 7 percent interest for a house. We have given you what your monthly payments would be if the loan was amortized over 30, 20, 15, and 10 years. Calculate how much that mortgage will cost you by the time you have paid it all off.

   Use the formula: Monthly payment multiplied by number of payments = total amount paid minus principal (amount borrowed) = cost of the mortgage.

   We've calculated the 10 year cost for you. You calculate the others.

   If this $100,000 mortgage is amortized over:

	10 yrs at 7%	15 yrs at 7%	20 yrs at 7%	30 yrs at 7%
Monthly payments	$1,161.08	$898.82	$775.30	$665.30
Amount paid at end of period	$139,329.60	_____	_____	_____
Cost of borrowing	$ 39,329.60	_____	_____	_____

   10 years: $1,161.08 x 120 payments   = 139,329.60 - 100,000
   = $39,329.60

   15 years: _____

   20 years: _____

   30 years: _____

2. Now think about these rates. The monthly payments are not that different between 10 and 20 year loans, but take a look at the difference in the amounts you end up paying! You pay a bit more each month and save a great deal of money!

   Which type of loan is the most cost effective?

month	balance x	rate =	interest +	principal =	payment
1	$100.00	1 percent	$1.00	$7.88	$8.88
2	92.12	1 percent	.92	7.96	8.88
3	84.16	1 percent	.84	8.04	8.88
4	76.12	1 percent	.76	8.12	8.88
5	68.00	1 percent	.68	8.20	8.88
6	59.80	1 percent	.60	8.28	8.88
7	51.52	1 percent	.52	8.36	8.88
8	43.16	1 percent	.43	8.45	8.88
9	34.71	1 percent	.35	8.53	8.88
10	26.18	1 percent	.26	8.62	8.88
11	17.56	1 percent	.18	8.70	8.88
12	8.86	1 percent	.09	8.86	8.95
Totals			$6.63	$100.00	$106.63*

You'll note that the last payment in the loan example is seven cents more than the others. The exact payment amount is somewhere between $8.88 and $8.89 and, since you can't pay fractions of a penny, lenders add up all the fractions and lump the total into the last payment. Now you see why lenders use computers to calculate the loan payments!

If this all looks a little confusing, that's because it is. Lenders use computers to calculate the interest and principal payments. The result: you pay back the loan in a succession of *equal* payments (except for that last one, as seen on the previous chart).

This is called an *amortized loan*. Amortized loans are repaid, or "put to death," in equal payments. (*Mortis* means death in Latin—as in *mort*uary and rigor *mortis*.)

Putting a loan "to death" sounds pretty painful. It is! Instead of *earning* interest, you're *paying* interest.

Compound Interest Loans

The above installment loan was a *simple interest* loan. You paid interest only on the principal—what you borrowed. There's another kind of loan available, and it's even worse.

In Chapter 2, How Banks Work, we described compound interest. Your bank pays you compound interest on your savings account. Each month you earn interest on the total balance: what you put in, plus all the interest you've earned so far. You earn interest on interest. Compound interest is a good thing when you're on the *receiving* end. It's no fun at all when you're *paying* it.

Most credit card accounts are compound interest loans in disguise. When you buy something with your credit card and don't pay the bill in full when it arrives, the issuer (lender) treats it as a loan and lets you pay it off monthly. If you do this a lot, you end up with a balance that can reach thousands of dollars.

Instead of making you pay off this loan in a certain amount of time (like an installment loan), the lender lets you make *minimum payments* each month. The amount of this small payment is printed on your bill, so it's pretty tempting to pay this little amount instead of paying off the whole thing. Here's the tricky part.

The interest you owe for that month may be *more* than the minimum payment. What do lenders do with the unpaid interest? They add it to your balance! The next month, you're not only paying interest on what you borrowed, you're paying interest on the interest.

What's more, you haven't even paid off much of the principal. So you still owe all of it. You're making payments on your credit card, yet the balance is going up! Believe it or not, it gets even worse.

If you are late with your payment, or go over your credit limit, you are charged a fee. You guessed it—they add that to the balance too. Now you're paying interest on *everything*.

It's a little like trying to climb a down escalator—except that you are headed down a down escalator and there's no way to get to the top. By the time you pay off your outrageous balance (if you ever do), you will have paid enough interest to buy two of whatever you bought in the first place.

It doesn't have to be this way. In the next chapter we'll show you how to keep a credit card under control.

Finding What's Fair

Lenders are in the business of renting money. And like any business, they do what they can to attract customers. Borrowing is enticing because it allows you to buy stuff you can't otherwise afford. Lenders capture your attention by emphasizing the "low monthly payments" and draw your attention *away* from all the extra money you're going to be paying in interest.

So how can you measure the true cost of a loan? Several years ago the U.S. Congress passed a law to help you out. The "Truth in Lending Act" requires lenders to state the terms of their loans in a standard format—kind of like the nutritional information required on food labels. There are some key terms to look for.

APR: The Annual Percentage Rate tells you the rate the lenders use to calculate the interest. They divide the APR by 12 to calculate your monthly interest charges.

Other Charges: These are fees and penalties you may have to pay for such things as annual fees, late payments, bounced checks, and early repayment of the loan. These things add up, so take note and take care.

Total of Payments: This is the most important number on the loan. When the loan is done and paid for, this is the amount you will have paid. This is a sobering figure when you compare it to the *cash price:* the difference between the two is the price you pay for using someone else's money.

Rewind

1. Lenders are in the money-rental business.

2. The "rental fee" is called interest. How they calculate the interest makes a big difference in how much you pay.

3. An installment loan uses simple interest. You pay interest only on the portion of the principal you haven't paid back yet.

4. An amortized loan is an installment loan that's paid off in equal monthly payments.

5. A compound interest loan charges interest on principal and any unpaid interest.

6. Most credit card accounts become compound interest loans if you don't pay your bill in full.

notes

_____
_____
_____
_____
_____
_____
_____
_____
_____
_____
_____
_____
_____
_____
_____
_____
_____
_____
_____
_____
_____
_____
_____
_____
_____

CHAPTER
8
Credit Cards

Chapter 8

Credit Cards

Are credit cards a curse or a blessing? They can be either, depending on how you use them. Let's take a look at how credit cards work, and then we'll show you how to use them as a blessing and avoid their many curses.

Technically speaking, the credit card is an incredible advancement in the world of finances. You can be in a store in London or Lisbon, St. Louis or Seattle, and if you have a credit card, you don't need cash. Just hand over the card, sign your name, and collect your merchandise.

Thirty or forty days later, you'll receive a printed statement itemizing your shopping spree. All you have to do is pay the bill. What could be easier?

It truly is simple and very convenient if (and that's a big IF) you pay the full amount on the statement as soon as it's received.

The problem begins with a tiny line on the statement: *Minimum Payment Due.* The number after those exhilarating words is awfully attractive—and a lot smaller than the number showing your total balance. In fact, it may be one of the most deliciously destructive traps ever devised. Once it catches you, it doesn't let go.

Interest Free—for Some

As we showed you in the previous chapter, credit card issuers make a bundle of money on interest when you fail to pay your balance in full. When you choose to pay off your balance in monthly payments, you automatically lose the "grace period," and you pay the maximum interest rate.

The grace period is the difference between the date you first make a purchase and the date your payment is due. If you pay the full amount within that period, there is a grace period, or free ride, with no interest charge—usually 25 or 30 days after the statement is printed. That's a good thing.

But this wonderful grace period applies only if you paid off last month's balance in full. If you had an unpaid balance from last month (i.e., you still owe money on the card), you're charged interest on any new purchases from the moment you make them. No grace period. No free ride. And for many, there's no way out.

If you pay the minimum payment amount, or any amount less than the full balance owed, you're charged interest on *everything*—old purchases, new purchases—and that interest is added *daily*.

What does that mean in real numbers? It's possible to borrow $1,000 on a credit card to buy something you *have to have*, only to end up paying over $2,000 when the balance is finally paid off. Such a deal!

As we pointed out before, credit cards themselves are not the problem. It's all in *how you use them*. If you use your credit card only to pay for things in your budget *and* you pay the balance in full every month, there's no problem. Do this, and you've got a convenient way to pay for things, to say nothing of an excellent credit record to help you in the future. That's a blessing.

Credit Card Practice

1. Ask your parents if you can use their credit card to buy the things you need and you have budgeted for this month.

2. Keep a record of everything you have used the card for.

3. When the credit card statement comes, get a copy of it and check the items on it to make sure your purchases are recorded correctly.

4. Repay your parents or actually make the payment to the bank. Make sure you can pay them back as soon as the statement comes in.

If You're a Student, You're a Target!

We know of a college student who obtained *28 credit cards*, which he frequently and proudly displayed to his female friends as a measure of his success. Although he was only 18 when he started his collection, he had the same name as his father, and he used that to his advantage—or, in this case, to his disadvantage. Before long he began to use one card to pay off another card, and by the time he reached his 20th birthday, this college student had accumulated nearly $10,000 in debt!

College-bound high school seniors are attractive targets for credit card issuers. Even if you have no established credit, lenders are eager to capture your loyalty—*and* your wallet. In fact, banks spend millions of dollars each year luring unwary students with special promotions: no-annual-fee cards, gold cards, frequent flyer miles, special discounts on new cars, and other incentives.

Taming a Wild Card

If you're not yet old enough to be a credit card target, you soon will be. Many students run into trouble within months of receiving their first credit card. If you should ever run out of control with plastic, the card won't be the one that needs to be tamed. It will be you and your buying habits. So, we want to give you some taming tricks.

1. Stop Now.

If you let a balance roll over into the next month, STOP THERE: Do not use your card again. Any new purchase gets hit with interest the moment you make it. Instead, pay off the old balance in full immediately so the interest doesn't start escalating. (It's surprising how many people forget that the way out of a hole is up, not down.)

2. Pay Now.

The dreaded interest is stacking up daily, so don't wait until your next statement to make a payment. As soon as you have the money, send the issuer a check with your card account number on it. The interest madness stops the day after they get your check. If you can't pay it off with one check, send them another one the following week. Do this until the account is back to zero. (Don't know what your balance is? Call them. That's what the 800 number on the statement is for.)

3. Flee from Fees.

See to it that your payments arrive before the deadline. If you miss it, you'll be hit with a fat late fee *and* interest on the account balance. If you know you're going to be late, call the issuer and tell them. Sometimes they'll cut you some slack—but only if they hear from you. (With creditors, absence doesn't make their hearts grow fonder—it grows *harder*.) If the check bounces, you're slammed with another fee. And if you go over your credit limit, you may be hit with still another penalty.

4. Toss the Offers.

When you open your statement and all those offers for insurance and merchandise fall out, dump them in the trash. You don't need what they're selling— and if you do you'll find it cheaper elsewhere.

5. Cancel.

When all else fails, destroy the card. When it comes down to a battle of who's controlling whom, concede the battle and cut up the card. A wild credit card habit is a sign that your budget and money management skills aren't healthy. Take a time-out from the credit game and work on the basics. You'll thank yourself later and get another card when you're ready.

We know what you're thinking. A few dollars in fees and interest isn't going to kill you. You're right . . . right now. But the card habits you establish will be with you for the rest of your life. Get it right, right from the start, and you'll be all right later on. But if you mess up at the start, you'll be fighting your bad habits (and your bad credit record) for years to come. We've seen the sad result of these habits in thousands of lives and we know that *now* is the best time for you to prevent financial disaster in your future.

So there you have it. A wisely managed credit card can be a real help to your money management and financial future. Or it can be a debt-trap that ensnares you now and holds you captive for years to come. Blessing or curse: The choice is yours!

Rewind

1. Credit cards are high-interest loans in disguise. If you fail to pay the balance in full every month, you're hooked into a loan.

2. The grace period is the number of days between a purchase and the date the payment is due. The grace period does not apply if the account has an unpaid balance from a previous month, or the current balance is not paid in full.

3. If a credit card habit gets out of hand, take immediate action to get it under control. Two or three months of a bad habit can lock you into years of debt.

notes

_____

_____

_____

_____

_____

_____

_____

_____

_____

_____

_____

_____

_____

_____

_____

_____

_____

CHAPTER
9

The Dangers of Borrowing

Chapter 9

The Dangers of Borrowing

Borrowing money has become a national pastime. Many Americans are in debt and spend much of their income trying to get out. This chapter will show you how to avoid loans you don't need and how to get a fair loan for things that matter.

Most Americans live on borrowed money. They "rent" other people's money to buy houses, cars, stereos, furniture, clothes, vacations—anything they can buy with a credit card or bank loan. Our government and many businesses operate the same way. But before you follow this well-traveled road into debt, you need to know what borrowing can do to your finances, relationships, and future. There are three traps that ensnare borrowers.

Borrowing Is Expensive

As we showed you earlier in the book, whenever you borrow money to buy something that goes down in value, you lose money. That's because you're *paying interest* and missing out on the opportunity to *earn interest* by putting those payments in your savings account instead. Meanwhile the thing you bought is depreciating (its value is decreasing).

Sometimes you actually have to make payments on something that's *worthless*: If you borrow money to pay for a cheap stereo or bad car, you may end up making monthly payments on it even after it's in the junk heap.

With very few exceptions, you are better off saving your money for something until you can pay cash. We'll talk about those in a bit.

Borrowing Is Addictive

When you borrow money, you're really borrowing from your future. Why? Let's say you want to buy a new car. That takes money. Most of us "buy" money with our time: we give our employers our time and they give us cash for it. If you had bought enough money with your time in the past, you could pay cash for that car today.

But you didn't buy enough cash with your time, or maybe you just spent too much of that cash on shoes, CDs, and cheeseburgers. Either way, you can't "quantum leap" back into the past to buy more money with your time. Those hours are gone.

There's only one place you can still turn your time into cash: the future. Those hours are not spent.

If you want to drive that new car today, you're going to have to borrow money from paychecks *you haven't earned yet.* So you borrow several thousand dollars from a bank and promise to pay them back with money you'll earn by selling your time on a job. You've just sold some of your future. If this is confusing, just wait. It's about to get depressing.

Flash forward a couple of years. You're now working those hours that you sold two years ago so you could ride around in a new car. Well, that new-car smell is gone, the tread is thinning on the tires, and the engine is making a funny rattling sound. But you can't fix these things because the money you earn is going straight to the bank to pay off the loan. So where do you go to find the money to fix your car? You guessed it: your future again. You borrow more money.

Most people live like this year after year. They spend *today* paying off the past; then they mortgage the *future* to pay for the things they want today. Don't get hooked by this addiction. With very few exceptions, if you can't afford to pay cash, you can't afford it.

Make today pay its own way. Then save a little extra to buy some freedom in your future.

Borrowing Is Destructive

If you get a loan and fail to repay it according to the terms of the agreement, the lender will pursue you until you repay the money. You'll be bombarded with phone calls and letters. This is not the kind of popularity you want. The lender also will report your delinquency to credit reporting agencies, so getting another loan (or an apartment or a job) may become nearly impossible.

Also, to force you to repay the loan, the lender can sue you in court. The judge can make you sell things you own to repay the debt, and he or she can *garnishee* your wages, which means your employer must deduct your payments straight out of your paychecks and you only get what is left. This judgment also will show up on your credit record. You get the picture—failing to repay a loan is disastrous not only to your credit but also to your freedom.

But wait—it can get worse. Even if you manage to make all your payments and avoid the wrath of the creditor, a burden of debt can interfere with a lot of things: your family, friendships, marriage, job, education, and personal life. Every dollar of debt is a commitment to a job. As your debt increases, so must your paycheck. That usually means more hours away from other priorities.

Some of these priorities will begin to suffer: your grades drop because you don't have time to study; the people you love get tired of never seeing you, so those relationships become strained; your spiritual life goes dry because you don't have time to go to church (or are too tired to make the effort). It's no coincidence that those with the biggest debts also have the most trouble in their marriages: money problems rank high on the list of reasons couples divorce.

Card Costs

Get a credit card form. Investigate the hidden cost to card use.

1. Let's say you have a card with 15 percent interest and a $1,000 balance on your card. How much would you be paying for that $1,000 if you only made $100 payments each month? Don't forget to include the credit card charges, which are often a yearly fee—for example, $25 plus interest charges.

    Here's how to calculate it: Your monthly interest is 15 percent divided by 12 months = 0.0125.

    Use the equation: balance minus payment = new balance + (new balance x interest) = next month's balance.

    Month   1: $1,000 - 100 = 900 + (900 x 0.0125) = $911.25
    Month   2: $911.25 -100 = 811.25 + (811.25 x 0.0125)
                    = 811.25 + 10.14 = $821.39
    Month   3: $821.39 -100 = 721.39 + 9.02 = $730.41
    Month   4: $730.41 - 100 = _____
    Month   5: _____
    Month   6: _____
    Month   7: _____
    Month   8: _____
    Month   9: _____
    Month 10: _____
    Month 11: _____
    Month 12: _____
          (don't forget to add $25 for the yearly user fee)
    Month 13: _____
    Month 14: _____

    How much do you end up paying for interest? Add up all the interest payments you have made. For a start: 11.25 + 10.14 + 9.02 + ...

    It's a significant amount.

2. What if you make payments of $500? (Use the same equation as above.)
    Month 1: _____
    Month 2: _____
    Month 3: _____

    This time your interest is very little.

    Now ask yourself, "Is credit card use worth it?"

    If you paid off the balance each month, that's an even better story!

*Every dollar of debt means more time away from the people
and pursuits that matter to you.*

How To Borrow Wisely

Despite the dangers of borrowing, there *are* times when a loan may be necessary. Some people find themselves in an emergency situation: they need a loan to pay for a place to live, or to pay for an operation, or to help a loved one in need.

Sometimes borrowing money is actually a wise financial move. If a loan enables you to make an *appreciating investment* (one that goes up in value), the money you make can offset the cost of the interest. For example, you might consider borrowing money to purchase a computer and printer if you are confident in your ability to make money as a writer or a graphic artist.

Many people borrow money to buy their houses, figuring that it's better to invest their rent money in something they can sell someday. And if real estate prices go up, they may make money, even after accounting for the interest they paid on the loan.

A good education also can be an appreciating investment. Many students borrow money through special student loans to pay for college. We'll talk more about student loans in a later chapter.

Tips for Using Loans

You can avoid much of the pain and pressure of debt by following our borrowing tips.

- Never borrow money needlessly. Avoid impulse purchases. Talk to parents and wise friends before making any large purchase.

- Remember that a loan doesn't lower a price tag: it raises it. And you will have to pay that higher price eventually. Even if you go bankrupt, you'll pay for it—with years of bad reputation, no credit, loss of freedom, and other painful losses, both financial and personal. To God, bankruptcy is not an answer. You've promised to pay your creditors and you need to keep your promises. In God's eyes you still owe the money.

- Be absolutely certain that the benefits of borrowing far exceed the cost of the loan and the restrictions it puts on your future.

- Be sure your purchase will last longer than the loan you need to buy it. You start losing money as soon as you sign a loan for anything that depreciates.

- If you have trouble making a payment, immediately contact your creditor. Explain the situation and work out a repayment arrangement. Do everything you can to save your credit rating.

Rewind

1. Borrowing is expensive: Instead of earning interest, you're paying it.

2. Borrowing is addictive: When a chunk of your money has to pay off things you bought in the past, there's less money to pay cash for what you want or need now. So you borrow more.

3. Borrowing is destructive: It can destroy your finances and your credit, and it could strain your relationships with family and friends.

4. Borrowing money for a house, education, or business can help you if the investment appreciates more than the cost of the loan.

5. If you use a credit card, pay the bill in full every month.

notes

notes

_____
_____
_____
_____
_____
_____
_____
_____
_____
_____
_____
_____
_____
_____
_____
_____
_____
_____
_____
_____
_____
_____
_____
_____

CHAPTER 10

How To Give Money Wisely

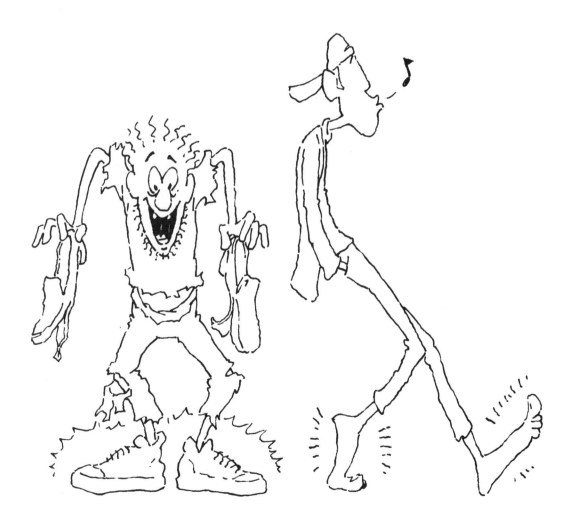

Chapter 10

How To Give Money Wisely

Everything you've learned so far has shown you how to take control of your money. Now that you've worked, earned, saved, budgeted, and accounted for all that money, we're going to show you how to give it away! Giving money to God is one of your greatest privileges—your gift to God. Get out your "wrapping paper."

Imagine you are in the following scenario. You've just landed the job of a lifetime. You've been appointed manager of a major account; you oversee the investment of *millions* of dollars of your boss's money. He's given you some instructions on the investments that he prefers, but he's entrusted you with free reign over the actual investments. He trusts you to make the right decisions. What a job!

This is not an imaginary situation. You already have this job. Your "boss," God, is the creator, ruler, and owner of all things. And He has chosen *you* to manage a portion of His wealth. Over your lifetime, you will handle millions of dollars—maybe *billions*. What you do with the money is *your* decision. It's a big job.

Fortunately, He's given you instructions (you can find them in the Bible) on how he wants you to invest His money. God is a great "boss," and His investment guidelines are designed to make your life fulfilling and rich. They may not make you rich with money, but they *will* make you rich in the things that count: faith, joy, friends, family, and the certainty that your life *matters*. God's instructions to you regarding His money are pretty simple. Let's take a look.

Instruction #1: Say Thanks

In the Old Testament, God told his people to *"Bring the whole tithe into the storehouse, so that there may be food in My house"* (Malachi 3:10). *Tithe* is an Old English word meaning "tenth." God told them to *give back* 10 percent of their wealth (back then, they gave livestock and crops) as a way of saying thanks for all that God had given them.

Nowadays, most people don't tithe with camels, cows, and corn. (For one thing, they don't fit in the offering container.) But people *do* give 10 percent of their wealth to God's house (their church) in money.

Tithing to your local church is an investment in the lives of the people in your community. The money you give pays for your ministers, the youth program, the building, your missionaries, and every ministry your church provides. It really counts!

Believe it or not, some folks tithe *more* than 10 percent. They may give 20 percent, 30 percent, or more! Sound crazy? It's not, really. They know it is God's money and they are just stewards (managers) of it. And, they also know that God always takes care of all their needs with what's left after they give to Him.

Let's say you've got a good job and you're making $40,000 a year. You tithe 10 percent: $4,000. You work hard, do well, get some raises, and pretty soon you're making $80,000. You want to thank God for the raises, so you tithe 20 percent: $16,000. You're still left with $28,000 more than you had before!

Of course, most people don't see it that way. They spend their extra money on bigger houses and faster cars, which just results in more carpets to vacuum and more speeding tickets to pay.

It works the other way too. For some people, to begin tithing an entire 10 percent is too much all at once. So they use a *graduated* tithe: They start smaller and work their way up as they are able.

If you think 10 percent is too big a chunk for you to give right now, start with 5 percent. God will honor your faithfulness and make it possible for you to give higher amounts in the future. As an act of faith, give 5 percent for two months; then increase it to 6 percent and then, a couple of months later, 7 percent. Work your way to 10 percent. You'll be so surprised at how this works, you may want to keep going! But you'll never know the thrill of saying thanks to God with a tithe unless you try. Do it this week.

Instruction #2: Help the Needy

One time Jesus was talking to some people who were pretty proud about their diligent tithing. He wasn't impressed. Instead, he let them know that while they were obeying the tithing instruction, they *"neglected the weightier provisions* [more important matters] *of the law: justice and mercy and faithfulness"* (Matthew 23:23).

Tithing is important. But it's just a start. Taking care of people in need is high on God's priority list. The church takes care of some people's needs, but there are many more needy people around than your local church can take care of.

Jesus told a powerful story about helping the needy. It leaves no doubt about the importance of this act of giving. *"For I was hungry and you gave Me something to eat; I was thirsty and you gave Me drink; I was a stranger, and you invited Me in; naked,*

Do a Bible Study on Tithing

1. Get a concordance and look up the following words. Write down key verses for each. Then write something the verses teach you about the terms.

    Tithe
    References: _____
    Notes: _____
    _____
    _____
    _____

    Giving
    References: _____
    Notes: _____
    _____
    _____
    _____

    Freewill Offering
    References: _____
    Notes: _____
    _____
    _____
    _____

    First Fruits
    References: _____
    Notes: _____
    _____
    _____
    _____

2. Calculate 10 percent of your weekly or monthly income. That's your tithe (or 10 percent).

3. Begin to tithe to your church. Take the money from your tithing/giving envelope each Sunday and put it in the offering plate.

4. Your church will give you a statement showing your total contributions once or twice a year.

and you clothed Me; I was sick, and you visited Me; I was in prison, and you came to me. . . . I say to you, to the extent that you did it to one of these brothers of Mine, even the least of them, you did it to Me" (Matthew 25:35–36,40).

If God feels the pain of every person in need, and that's a *lot* of pain, imagine the *joy* he feels when you help someone! Many teenagers give to others every month (and thus, to God). They may give regular gifts of money to homes for unwed mothers; or they support ministries to inner-city kids; or they sponsor needy kids overseas with monthly contributions and letters back and forth.

Take a look inside your heart. If there is a little voice telling you that you should respond, answer your heart by giving to the needy. That's another way to show God how grateful you are to be appointed a manager of his wealth.

Instruction #3: Give From Your Riches

In Luke, chapter 15, Jesus told a story about a rich farmer who was making plans to build some big barns to store all his harvest. (Back then, crops were like money, so barns were like bank vaults.) He figured, with all that wealth stored up in his barns, he could kick back and live like the rich and famous.

But God said to him, *"You fool! This very night your soul is required of you; and now who will own what you have prepared? . . . But seek for His kingdom and these things shall be added to you. . . . For where your treasure is, there will your heart be also"* (Luke 12:20,31,34).

Helping People in Need
AIDS hospices
Bible distribution programs
Bible translation ministries
Camping ministries
Child sponsorship
Day care programs
Drug and alcohol treatment programs
Evangelism ministries
Homeless ministries
Homes for abused children
Homes for battered women
Homes for unwed mothers
Hospitals
Hunger relief organizations
Inner-city ministries
Mission organizations
Pregnancy counseling centers
Prison ministries
Rehabilitation ministries
Shut-in ministries
Soup kitchens

When God calls somebody a fool, it's wise to sit up, pay attention, and figure out why! God had just blessed this guy with a great crop. But instead of figuring out how he could share this blessing with others, his only plan was to build a bigger place so he could keep it all to himself for the rest of his life (which wasn't long!). It was like a slap in God's face.

When God blesses you big, give big! When you receive riches, give from your riches. That brings up an important question: What are *riches*? The answer is not a dollar figure. You may make $1,200 in one year and consider yourself rich. But an adult in America making $12,000 a year is considered to be living on a poverty level. And some people with $12,000 *million* are trying to figure how to make more.

You've got *riches* when the bills are paid, you have food, clothing, and a place to live—and you still have some money left over to help other people.

When you get a new job, or a raise, or a big birthday check from your Aunt Edna, count your blessings. Don't do what that foolish farmer did. Say thanks to God again and give him back a bigger share—above your tithe.

Instruction #4: Sacrifice

"Let the man who has two tunics [coats] share with him who has none; and let him who has food do likewise" (Luke 3:11).

Here's another story from Jesus. He was watching some rich people put money in the collection basket. Then he saw a poor widow put in a couple of small coins. He said, *"This poor widow put in more than all of them; for they all out of their surplus put into the offering; but she out of her poverty put in all that she had to live on"* (Luke 21:3–4).

Jesus knows what it means to give till it hurts: He suffered great hurt when he was giving His own *life*. He also knows that sacrificial giving *changes* people. It does several things: Their faith increases, their love for others deepens, and they begin to understand the outrageous, unstoppable, unbelievable, incredible love God has for them (as well as anyone can really grasp such a thing).

We can teach you budgeting and accounting and check writing, but sacrificial giving is one of those things you just have to learn on your own. It's a spiritual thing, not a financial thing. It's giving up your wants to meet someone else's need. For example, you could share your lunch with someone who doesn't have one. Or you could give up an after-school job to volunteer at a day care center for underprivileged kids. You could give up some of your recreation time to visit someone who is in the hospital or in a nursing home.

You might ask, "But if I give up food, or clothing, or some other basic need, won't I end up suffering?" Jesus answered that question in the verse we just read from Luke in the last instruction. It's also in another place in the Bible: *"But seek first His kingdom and His righteousness; and all these things shall be added to you"* (Matthew 6:33).

When people give up their own needs to help others, they do so because Jesus lives in their hearts; and He says, "Trust me." And they do.

What Happens When You Give

- You say, "Thanks, God!"

- You help people who really need it.

- Your gift could help someone meet Jesus.

- You get to work for the God of the universe.

- You can be satisfied in knowing that you're doing what God says.

- You get to change the world.

- The church has been succeeding for 2,000 years. You are helping it to continue for another year.

- You're being a good steward of what God has given you.

- You're acting on your confidence that God will care for your needs because He loves you.

- You're treating others generously— the way God treats you.

If you're ready to take that risk, ask God to show you what sacrificial gift you can give and to whom. It might hurt, but it also will feel good.

A Different Set of Rules

There are many other instructions in the Bible, of course. If you read through the Gospel of Luke, you'll find dozens. All of God's money instructions are manageable, and every one of them will make your life better. Unfortunately, not everyone follows these instructions.

In fact, our culture teaches and lives by money rules that are often the *opposite* of God's instructions. But if you look within your church and your community, you'll find some people who follow the Book of Instruction (the Bible). They are thanking God, helping the needy, sharing their riches, and sacrificing. As a result, they are rich where it counts. They are changing the lives of others, and God is applauding their faithfulness. As money managers, they are doing a *good* job.

Making a Commitment

The first step to giving is to decide to tithe. Figure how much money you get per month, on average (from a full-time job, part-time work, or an allowance). If you're working from a weekly budget, base it on your weekly average. Then you must decide what *percentage* of your income you want to give back to God.

Now multiply your average income by that percentage; the result is the amount you will tithe. That's the amount of money you commit to give each month (or week).

Before you make the commitment, talk to God! Ask Him to help you decide on the amount of your commitment; and ask Him to help you have the discipline to carry through on it. If you're ready, you can fill in and sign the following commitment.

EXAMPLE:

TITHING 10 PERCENT ON $120 AVERAGE MONTHLY INCOME.

Average monthly income:	$120
Tithe (10 percent):	x .10
	————
Monthly tithe commitment:	$ 12

Dear Lord,

Thank you for caring for me in big and small ways. Thank you for providing me with food, clothes, and a place to live.

Thank you for providing me with an average income of $___ per _____. By signing this note, I'm acknowledging that I'm not the owner of this money; You are. You've appointed me manager of this money and all the other things you have given to me.

I'm grateful to you for my position. To acknowledge that it's your money, and to thank you for the opportunity to manage it, I'm committed to return _____ percent to you on a regular basis for _____ months.

This amounts to $_____ per _____.

Your servant, _____

Date: _____

Rewind

1. God is the owner of all things. He's appointed you to be manager of some of it.

2. The Bible contains God's instructions regarding His money.

3. God wants us to give back a portion of what He's given to us, as a way of saying thanks. This form of giving to the church is called a tithe.

4. God wants us to give to the needy. Their pain is His pain, and their joy is His joy.

5. God wants us to give even more from our riches, to thank Him richly when He blesses us richly.

6. God wants us to give sacrificially, which increases our faith, our love for others, and our understanding of His great love for us.

notes

_____

_____

_____

_____

_____

_____

_____

_____

_____

_____

_____

_____

_____

_____

notes

_____

_____

_____

_____

_____

_____

_____

_____

_____

_____

_____

_____

_____

_____

_____

_____

_____

_____

_____

_____

_____

_____

_____

_____

_____

How To Make Money with Money

Chapter 11

How To Make Money with Money

One of the best reasons for setting aside money for savings is that you can use that money to make more money. It's time to tell your money to "Go to work!" This chapter shows you how.

If you keep a good budget, you've got a *Long-Term Savings account*. Each week or month, you deposit a portion of your earnings into a savings account. Now let's learn some tips that will help you to make the most of these savings: How to make even more money with your money.

Always keep in mind the reasons for making more money: It's good stewardship; you'll be able to use that money to meet future needs, including financing God's plan for your life (college, trade school, marriage, mission field); and you'll have more money available to meet the needs of those around you.

Tip #1: Don't Invest In Things That Depreciate (Go Down in Value)

The money in your savings account is an *appreciating* investment. It's value is going up because you're *earning interest*. You're making money. If you withdraw some of that money to buy a pair of shoes, CDs, or sunglasses, you've now made a *depreciating* investment. Its value goes down the moment you walk out the store. You are losing money.

Let's say you buy a portable stereo for $100. A year later, the stereo is worth about $25 when you sell

Personal Stereo	
new price	$100
used price	- 25
depreciation	= $75
opportunity cost	+ $ 5
Total Cost (1 year)	= $80

it to your little brother. You got a year's worth of music out of it. (Actually, you only used it ten times because you couldn't afford to keep replacing the batteries, but let's not quibble.) Let's count the cost.

A year's worth of use cost you $75. The difference between what you paid for it and what you sold it for is called *depreciation*. It's a polite way of saying you lost money.

But wait, there's another loss. You *could* have put the $100 in a long-term savings account instead. If you had done that, you might have earned about $5 in interest. You missed out on that opportunity because you invested in the stereo. This $5 is called *opportunity cost*. Let's add it up: $75 in depreciation plus $5 in opportunity cost equals $80. Your year of stereo use cost $80 from savings.

Now $80 may not seem like a big deal. But in a few years, that $80 would have earned even more interest, so the loss would be about $100. And if you get in the habit of using your savings account for depreciating investments, there won't be enough money in there when it's time to buy a car or pay for college.

Spending your savings on depreciating items is like trying to walk up the *down* escalator—like we talked about in chapter 7. You have to work twice as hard to get to the top. Keeping your money in the savings account is like standing on the *up* escalator. You get to the top much faster, with less effort.

The simple point we are making is this: Use the money in your *long-term* savings account for *appreciating* investments. Use the money in your *short-term* savings or *spending account* to buy things that go down.

Tip #2: Never Borrow Money To Pay for Things That Depreciate

The fastest way to lose money is to buy a depreciating item with *borrowed* money. Let's buy that personal stereo again but, this time, pay for it with a credit card. You lose $75 in depreciation either way. And there's still an opportunity cost because your monthly payment ate up the money you usually set aside for savings. Those small, monthly deposits would have *earned* about $3 in interest. So, you see: Borrowing money still attacks your savings.

Then there's a *finance charge*. By the time you paid off the credit card balance (you took all year), you paid about $10 in interest. Your stereo cost $88. Now that may not seem like a lot.

Unfortunately though, most people buy a lot of other depreciating items with borrowed money: cars, furniture, TVs, vacations, *big* stereos—anything that can be charged on plastic or financed with a loan. They end up paying *thousands* of extra dollars in finance charges (interest). In some cases, they're still paying for a item long after it is broken or outdated!

Personal Stereo	
new price	$100
used price	- $25
depreciation	= $75
opportunity cost	+ 3
interest	+ 10
Total Cost (1 year)	= $88

When you buy a depreciating item with borrowed money, you're standing on the *down* escalator. You will *never* get to the top that way.

What's the solution? If you must buy a depreciating item, don't borrow the money. Instead, put a portion each month from your spending money into short-term savings. Then buy it when you have enough to pay *cash*.

Tip #3: Save Every Month

Some people wait until they're making lots of money before putting money into a savings account. But when that time comes, they have no savings habits. They continue to do what they've *always* done: cash the paycheck, spend all the money, and have nothing left to save for later.

Now is the time to start saving a percentage of every dollar you earn. Those regular weekly or monthly deposits do two things: First, they teach you a habit you'll be thankful for—for the rest of your life! Second, they *add up*! Those small monthly

deposits will grow as your income grows. In a few years, those deposits, plus the interest, will buy you a clean used car, help you through college, or get you started in your own business.

Whatever your income, you can put a portion of it into savings.

Try Investing

1. Create a mock investment portfolio for yourself. Most banks have a youth program with its own financial advisor who can meet with you to discuss the various banking and financial options available to you: registered savings, mutual funds, stock market. You can discuss minimum account deposits, different savings accounts and their interest rates, investment options and their time commitments, etc. (Allocate only a small amount, perhaps 10 percent of your total investment capital, for the stock market; it is a high risk.).

2. Before you do invest in different banking or investment plans, track them ON PAPER. Pretend you invested a portion of your income among the investments you feel are the best. Keep track on paper of how your investments would have done over several months if you really had committed your money. How did you do? Remember, plan and think before you commit.

Certificates of Deposit

Up to now, we've been talking about putting your money into a basic savings account. Did you know that banks offer other kinds of accounts that pay better interest? However, in exchange for the higher interest, the bank expects more from you: a higher balance, or a longer commitment, or both.

One of these types of accounts is called a *certificate of deposit*, or CD (not to be confused with the ones you play on your stereo, of course). When you put your money in a certificate of deposit (CD), you promise the bank that you won't withdraw it for a certain amount of time: six months, a year, or even longer. If you do decide to take the money out before the time is up, the bank will charge you. Maybe you've heard the ad: "a substantial penalty for early withdrawal."

Making a commitment to keep your money in a CD for a certain length of time can be a good thing. If you're often tempted to withdraw money from your savings account, putting it in a CD will lock it up for safekeeping. However, it's not wise to put *all* your savings in a CD. If an emergency comes up while it's locked away, you'll have to pay that penalty to get it out. Then you are back to losing money.

Banks also insist that you deposit a larger amount in a CD: $500 or $1,000 minimum. If you would like to open a CD but don't have that much money, there's a way to make it happen. Get an investment partner—a friend or relative—to open the account *with* you: Each of you contributes half the minimum deposit. When the CD *matures* (the time is up), you can split the balance, or "roll it over" (put it back into another CD).

On your next visit to the bank (make it this week!), ask about CDs: minimum deposits, interest rates, and yields (remember those?). If you have the minimum, or can manage to get the minimum with the help of an investment partner, consider putting some of your long-term savings into a CD.

U.S. Savings Bonds

Savings bonds are another way to put your money to work. A savings bond is like a loan to the government. You lend your money to the United States; then they pay it back, with interest, a few years later. Like a CD, your money is locked up for a while (typically a minimum of five years). You can keep it as long as you want and get your money back, with interest, whenever you need it.

If you are saving money for college, a savings bond can help. If you buy a bond now, you won't be able to cash it until you're in college. It will be worth more money exactly when you *need* more money.

Other Investments

If you've ever looked through the finance section of a newspaper, you know that there are many other kinds of investments: stocks, bonds, mutual funds, futures, and so on. The safest investments are with banks and the government (savings accounts, CDs, U.S. savings bonds). These institutions guarantee your investment: You won't *lose* money. But there's a definite drawback: They also pay the lowest interest.

With most other investments, there's the risk that you may lose money. For example: If you buy stock in a company that goes bankrupt, your stock is worthless, and you *lose*. But if the company prospers, you can sell your stock for more than you paid, and you *gain*.

There's a pretty reliable rule: The greater the potential for gain, the greater the risk. Investments that can earn the most money can also lose the most money.

Right now, as you're just starting to accumulate savings for your future, it's best to stick to the safe investments. There's no sense in risking your future on a bad stock investment. Keep your money in a savings account. If you can afford the minimum deposits and time restrictions of other bank accounts, such as CDs, put some money in them. And if you can afford to lock some away for five years, buy a savings bond.

You've worked hard for your money. Be sure it works hard for you.

Rewind

1. Avoid spending money on things that go down in value.

2. Don't borrow money to pay for things that go down in value.

3. Make regular deposits to your savings.

4. Certificates of deposit (CDs) pay higher interest in exchange for your commitment to keep the money in the bank longer.

5. U.S. Savings Bonds are loans to the government that pay you principal and interest in the future.

6. Bank and government investments are guaranteed not to lose money.

7. With most investments, the greater the potential for gain, the greater the risk of loss.

notes

_____

_____

_____

_____

_____

_____

_____

_____

_____

_____

_____

notes

Money Matters for Teens

CHAPTER 12

How To Spend Money

Chapter 12

How To Spend Money

You now have a carefully crafted budget and an account system to maintain your budget. In this chapter you'll learn some tricks and tips that will help you get the most out of every dollar in your spending account. Let's go shopping!

The Selling Game

Imagine a board game called *Consumer Madness*. Players in the game are divided into two groups. Those in the first group are called *sellers*; those in the second group are called *consumers*. The sellers compete with each other to get all the consumers' money by selling them their merchandise. The sellers compete with each other to spend the least amount of money on what they buy.

The game gets pretty wild: The sellers are shouting "Buy from me! You need what I have! You can't afford not to have it! It's on sale! Big discounts! Low prices!"

Meanwhile, the consumers are shopping around, deciding what they want, and spending all their money before the end of the game. Then they borrow more money and spend that too.

In this game, the consumers usually lose.

You guessed it: *Consumer Madness* isn't a board game. It's a *real* game, being played every day in America with real money. The sellers are the tens of thousands of companies that market all kinds of items to people: shoes, clothes, music, movies, food, candy, drinks, deodorant, makeup, magazines, sports equipment, stereos, and computer games.

These marketers spend *billions* of dollars in advertising. They sponsor TV shows, publish magazines, conduct giant marketing surveys, and employ hundreds of people to figure out how to get *you* to buy their products. It's no wonder that they're winning!

Most teenagers (and adults, for that matter) don't have nearly as much skill at *buying* as the marketers have at *selling*. It's a lopsided game. However, you can make the game more fair. By learning how the marketers play *their* side of the game, you can improve your performance on *your* side of the game. The result? You'll have more money to do more things, and you'll *take control* of your finances, buying decisions, and values.

There are tricks that are common to most marketers that they use to get you to buy something. They want you to believe you are getting what you want at the best price.

Keeping Track

1. Carry a small notebook.

2. For a month, write down everything you spend, no matter how small.

3. This means everything: gum, soft drinks, snacks, bus fare, comics, arcade games, as well as larger purchases.

4. Even if you are spending "loose" change, write it down.

You'll be amazed at how much you spend on little things or things you hardly think about or notice at the time. This exercise can help you feel in control of your money so you know exactly where it's all going, and you'll know exactly what you got for it so you can make adjustments to meet your priorities.

Trick #1: Big Discount!

The most common selling lure is to play with prices. To understand price tricks, first you need to understand what *price* means. In many countries the government and big businesses regulate or "fix" prices for things.

That means, for example, that a loaf of bread with a fixed price will cost the same no matter where you shop. If they set a fixed price on milk, a gallon will cost the same everywhere. And if they fix the price on music CDs, shopping around for the best price is a waste of time—they are the same in all the stores. The U.S. is *not* like that.

With very few exceptions, regulating or "fixing" prices is illegal in America. We have what economists call a "free-market economy." It's a fancy way of saying that people are free to sell things at whatever price they want. That means that a company that makes CD players can offer their merchandise to retail stores at whatever price they choose. Likewise, a store can offer to sell CD players to consumers at whatever price it chooses.

In either case, if the price is too high, people won't buy their CD players. So they try to come up with a price that is low enough for people to buy and high enough to cover their costs and make a profit.

When an electronics store advertises CD players at a "25 percent discount," your first question should be, "What price are they discounting?" Typically, they're saying that their price is 25 percent less than the *suggested retail price*. What's *that*? The suggested retail price (SRP) is a price the manufacturer comes up with. It's *suggested* because it's illegal for the manufacturer to *demand* retailers to sell things at a certain price. (A free market means they are free to set their own prices.)

The suggested retail price isn't a very official number. Almost no store sells a popular item at that price: They just use that price so they can claim that their actual price is so much lower!

That's just the beginning. The "25 percent discount" doesn't *have* to be based on the suggested retail price. Let's say that the SRP from the manufacturer for this particular CD player is $100. If it wants to, the store can offer the CD player for $150! They'll sell a few of them at that price to people who don't know enough to shop around. The next week, the store can mark down the price a whopping 25 percent—and sell them for $112.50. Meanwhile, a store down the street is offering the same CD player "on sale" for the same 25 percent discount, except that their discount is based on the $100 SRP. Their price: $75!

Sound deceiving? It is. Here's how to cut through the confusion: Ignore "Suggested Retail Price." Ignore "On Sale!" and "Marked Down!" and "Discount!" Just compare the real, walk-out-the-door prices. The rest is just marketing hype.

Flexible Price Tags	
PRICE	WHAT IT MEANS
wholesale price (cost)	what the manufacturer charges the retailer; it varies with supply and demand and quantity ordered
manufacturer's suggested retail price (MSRP)	what the manufacture claims the product is "worth"; typically used by retailer as a base for discounts
sale price, discount price	marketing hook used by retailers to encourage sales; may be a low price or simply a discount from an inflated price
real price	what it actually costs you to buy the product

Trick #2: Buy Now!

The quickest way to get you to buy something is to not let you have time to think about it first. The supermarket check stand is a great example. You know you shouldn't buy that candy bar; you are there to buy groceries. But it's practically *jumping* off the shelf.

If you had time to think about it, you'd say, "No, I don't need it." But the checker is just about to total your purchases, so you throw it on the checkout counter and pay for it without thinking. (And if you're *really* impulsive, you also bought a worthless tabloid with the headline, "ELVIS SPOTTED ON MARS.")

Sellers do all sorts of things to get you to buy before you've had a chance to think about it. They crowd their checkout stands with junk food and trinkets. They display candy and toys on low shelves so impulsive "cart jockeys" (little kids in shopping carts) will see and grab. They tell you there's a "limited quantity" so you'll buy it immediately, without considering the cost. (Hint: Except for God's love, there's a limited quantity to *everything!*)

For the same reason, sellers offer one-day and weekend sales, or tell you they'll give you a "special deal"—*if* you buy today. They know that if you walk out of the store, you may decide you don't need it after all.

There's nothing wrong with these tactics; if you owned a store you'd want to increase your sales too. But right now you're a consumer, not a seller, so it's smart to know how to resist impulse buys. Try the following tips.

- Keep your hands in your pockets in the checkout line. It works!

- Carry only enough money each day to cover your *needs*. You can't buy what you can't pay for.

- Set a "7 over 7" rule: Before buying anything that costs over $7, you must wait seven days. If you still want it a week later, you can buy it.

- When a salesperson pressures you with the fact that there are "only a few left," tell that person you'll leave the item so someone who needs it more than you do can buy it.

Trick #3: Save!

Sellers know that many people feel a little guilty when they spend money. And just about everyone feels good when they get a good deal. So they distract you from how much you're *spending* and congratulate you on how much you're *saving*. This is where the "discount price" really comes in handy. The old price was $100, the new price is $75: "Save $25!"

Let's set things straight. You're not *saving* anything. You're spending. You may be spending *less*, but you're still spending. The only time you're saving is when your money is in your savings account.

When you see those red tags showing the amount of money you're saving, ignore them. Look at the price. That's what you're going to *spend*, and that's what counts in your budget.

Rewind

1. Sellers are very serious in their efforts to get you to part with your money. Good money management can help you hold onto more of your money and get better deals on what you spend.

2. Sellers may set a higher price, then use it to claim that the *real* price is a discount. Ignore the percentages and compare real prices.

3. Sellers often arrange merchandise and make limited-time and limited-quantity offers to encourage impulse buying. Control your impulsive nature by putting off buying decisions until you've had time to think about it.

4. Sellers can distract you from how much you're spending by focusing on how much you're "saving." Ignore what you're "saving." Think instead of what you will be *spending*.

notes

_____

_____

_____

_____

_____

_____

How To Buy a Car

Chapter 13

How To Buy a Car

As a teenager, buying a car may be your first big investment. It may also be your first big financial disaster. However, it doesn't have to be that way. If you have a steady job and a good budget, you can buy a car that won't hold you hostage to car payments and repair bills. We will tell you how.

Visit any car dealership and you'll find a special lot for used cars. Take a walk down the rows of those used cars (also referred to as "previously owned" cars) and you're likely to see several cars that look brand new. If those shiny cars could talk, at least one of them would tell you how it was bought by a hopeful teenager who couldn't survive the first year of car payments. When the young owner of this once-new car missed a few payments, the bank took back the car. And all the money that went into the down payment and monthly payments was *lost.*

When you buy a new car, its value drops 30 to 40 percent the moment you drive it off the lot. That's an expensive drive! It can take *years* of monthly payments before you can sell that car for more than the amount you still owe on the loan.

Even if you can manage the car payments, the price of a new car may cost you in other areas. For example, you can spend all summer working to pay for your fancy new car. Or you can buy a good used car and use the money you "save" to pay for a trip to Germany (or, better yet, to make all of the payments). Big car payments translate into more time at work and less time and money for other things.

That's why we usually recommend buying a used car. Let someone else pay the premium for that new-car smell. Of course, buying a used car can be risky too. You don't know much about the car except what the seller tells you, and he or she may not be trustworthy. If you're able to find someone who likes to buy a new car every year but has taken good care of his or her vehicle, that would be a wise buy.

Failing that, you'll need to do some work to get a good deal. The investment is worth it. The time you spend hunting for the right deal is recovered in the time you won't be spending at the repair shop and *won't* be spending at work to pay for the repairs.

Research Project

The first step to buying a car is to do your research. Go to the library and look through the consumer information on used cars. There you'll find guides listing every car make, model, and year and the results of surveys taken by their owners. These surveys help you to identify cars that are reliable and inexpensive to maintain. This is important: An unreliable car can cost you as much in repair bills as the payments on a new car.

After you've picked out a few reliable models that match your preferences, you need to study the marketplace. Study the classified ads for a few weeks. Read the ads on the models you're looking for. Get a feel for the prices sellers are asking. Make calls to some of these sellers and ask about the mileage and condition of their cars. After a while, you'll start to get a sense of what's available and what you'll have to pay.

Car Dating

Now you're ready to go shopping. Buying a used car is like getting married: In either case, you'd better learn all you can about your "partner" before you take the plunge. But when you're "courting" a car, you have just one or two opportunities to get to know it before you "tie the knot," so you have to find out all you can very quickly.

Make some "dates" by calling the phone numbers in a few car ads that interest you. Take a knowledgeable friend or family member with you when you go to "meet" these cars. At each of your appointments, take a close look at the car: check under the hood, look beneath the car, take a test drive, and test the equipment. By checking out a few cars in this way, you can get a better sense of each car's strengths and weaknesses.

You also can learn about a car by talking to the person who knows it best: the owner. Ask lots of questions. The car can't speak for itself, so you need to interview the one person who's most qualified to speak for it. Remember, you're thinking about giving up thousands of your hard earned dollars to this person—you want as much information as you can get. Ask about the car's history, how long the owner has had it, why he or she is selling it, and so on. (See box at right for more questions.)

The answers are important, but so is the conversation. You can learn a lot about a car by studying the *owner*. If the owner doesn't know many answers or seems unwilling to talk about the car in detail, he or she may be trying to hide something. If it's about the car's history, he or

Ask the Seller . . .

How long have you owned the car?

Why are you selling it?

What repairs has it had, and when?

What equipment has been replaced?

Has it been in any accidents?

Has it ever been broken into?

Does it leak oil?

What kind of gas mileage does it get?

When was the last tune-up?

When were the tires replaced?

Who does the maintenance?

Is the car paid off?

If not, who is the lienholder?

she will have a tough time keeping up the lie as you ask more questions (lies often unravel in the details). If you sense that the seller isn't trustworthy, move on.

If the car and owner seem reliable, thank the seller for his or her time and explain that you have some other cars to look at. Then check out more cars. Avoid making any deal or negotiating until you've looked at several cars. Walking away helps you to make a more thoughtful decision, and it tells the seller that you are not desperate. If an aggressive seller senses urgency, he or she will turn on the pressure to sell and will be much less willing to negotiate the price.

Getting "Engaged"

After checking out several cars, you may find one you want to spend time with. Make another date to check out the car. Take along someone who knows cars pretty well, because you want to give the car a thorough examination. After all, if you're going to buy the whole car, you should know everything about it. Listed below are some things to do, but you also may want to drive the car to a mechanic for a check-up. That examination may run you $50 or more, but it can be a good investment if you're unsure of your ability to spot problems yourself.

If the car seems mechanically sound, make an offer. This is when the fine art of negotiating comes into play. Like many financial deals, there are often three prices in a car deal:

asking price — what the seller is asking for
bidding price — what the buyer is offering to pay
final price — what you agree on

Sellers typically set their asking prices by looking through the ads to learn what other similar cars are selling for. That's why it's important for you to read those ads yourself. You need to have a feel for prices to know if the asking price is reasonable. Smart sellers know that buyers will try to negotiate the prices downward, so they often jack up the prices to give them room to come down.

Savvy buyers do the same thing: They lower their bid a little to give them room to come up. If each of you have done your homework, the price you settle on will be somewhere in the middle of your two prices. Sometimes sellers ask for "firm" prices, which means they don't want to negotiate.

Car Examination

- Test all the lights: headlamps, tail lamps, backup lights, brake lights, turn signals.

- Test the radio and all its knobs and features.

- Test windshield wipers and washer in all settings.

- Test the fan, heater, air conditioner, defroster, and all vents and switches.

- Turn the key to the first position and check all gauges and warning lights.

- Try out all other dashboard features: switches, levers, ashtray, lighter, glove compartment door.

- Run all the windows up and down.

- Adjust the seats in all positions; check beneath them and beneath floor mats.

- Try all the doors, check the locks; open and latch the trunk and hood.

- Feel the antenna, mirrors, gas filler door and cap, and all trim to make sure they're secure.

- Look for paint that doesn't match or has a different texture (signs of body repair after an accident).

- Check for covered-up body rust by looking and feeling inside wheel wells.

- Pull up any floor mats in trunk; check spare tire.

- Examine tires for uneven tread wear or low pressure.

- Check beneath car for wet brake hoses and oil dripping from engine, transmission, and differential.

- Look at the driveway or parking spaces near the car for oil stains, which might indicate that the car leaks oil.

- Check engine for fresh oil, loose hoses, or wires.

- Check for an engine that's "too clean"—a sign that it may have a major leak that's merely been cleaned away rather than repaired.

- Look through repair records to see what's been fixed or replaced; do they match owner's story?

- Check the owner's registration and title to be sure the car is registered and owned by the person selling it to you. (If the car isn't paid for, the title will show a "lien holder," which means that the bank still has an interest in the car and must sign the title to make the sale.)

If the sellers' price is higher than another similar car in the same condition, you can say something like this: "I'm interested in the car, but your price is higher than another car I'm interested in, so I need to take another look at the other car and see if it's worth the difference." Be certain that you always tell the truth. God will honor that.

At that point, the seller may decide that the price is not so firm after all and will be willing to match or beat the other seller's price. If not, that's okay too. Say thank you and tell the seller you'll be back if you decide on his or her car. That gives you a "time out" to consider your decision.

"Tying the Knot"

When you've settled on the car you want and the price you and the seller can agree on, you need to make the deal. It's generally unwise to walk around with thousands of dollars in cash, so offer to make a $100 deposit to hold the deal till you can get a cashier's check from the bank. Unless the seller has had lots of calls on the car, he or she generally will accept your deposit. Be sure to have him sign a receipt.

(date)

One hundred dollars ($100) received from

_____ *(your name) as a deposit on the purchase of*
_____ *(make, model and year of car) for* _____ *(total sales price).*
Balance is due by _____ *(tomorrow's date, or whatever you agree to).*

Hold on to this receipt—it's your proof the car is being held for you and will not be sold to someone else who might come along with a better offer. Now it's time to go to the bank and get a certified or cashier's check to pay for the car. Be sure to list the owner's name on the bank check. If you leave it blank, it's like cash: lose it and whoever finds it is the proud owner of your money and you will have nothing—no car and no money.

When you return with the big check, be sure the owner writes out a bill of sale, which should list the date, your name, the seller's name, the vehicle identification number, and the price. The owner also will need to sign over the title of the car. You'll need the bill of sale and signed title to register the car at the motor vehicle department.

Congratulations! You've just bought a car.

More Buying Tips

As we said earlier, buying a good used car for a good price takes some work. But if you do your homework, you'll get the right car—and may even enjoy the whole process. Try the following buying tips.

- *Bring a friend.* When you negotiate a deal, it's best to have a knowledgeable friend or family member come with you. Sometimes the thrill of buying a car can get to your head and make you agree to something you shouldn't. A friend can help you to consider your decision more carefully.

- *Don't carry cash.* When shopping for a used car, some people carry the cash on them. They figure that they'll be able to make a better deal if they do it on the spot. But if the seller knows you've got the cash on you, you appear to be very eager to do a deal. That's bad for negotiating. And it's never wise to walk around with that much money.

- *Check out the seller.* If you can, arrange to see the car at the seller's home. A person who keeps his or her house and personal appearance in order is more likely to treat the car the same way. A seller who's just passing through town, or not living at a fixed address, is less likely to sell you a car you'd want. At his or her home, you can also look for oil stains on the pavement—a sign that the car may leak oil.

- *Watch for registration problems.* Check out the car's registration, safety inspection sticker, or smog certification. A car without these things will cost you a bundle when it's time to register. Also beware of out-of-state cars: you may have to pay several hundred dollars to refit the car to pass your state's standards. This is especially true if you live in California.

- *Check the mileage.* Some people turn back the mileage on their odometers. If a car has low miles but worn-out pedal pads and floor mats, something may be fishy. Also, if a repair record shows a mileage reading greater than the odometer's, something's crooked.

- *Walk away from pressure.* If the seller is putting pressure on you to buy immediately, don't give in. If someone else shows up to make an offer while you're looking at the car, don't get into a bidding war. The other buyer may not be genuine, and even if he or she is, you'll do better to wait and make an unpressured decision. Call back the next day and see if the car is still available.

- *Avoid car lots.* Car dealers must jack up the price to cover their overhead, so their prices are generally higher than private sellers (you can confirm this fact by looking through the car ads). And since they're not the owner, they probably know very little about the car's history. Some dealers offer a short warranty, but chances are they've already fixed any problems that might arise during that short period. They won't tell you about more expensive problems that may occur later.

Your Car Budget

If you've managed to buy a car without taking out a loan, you've accomplished a major step in financial freedom. But the Auto account in your budget must also cover insurance, repairs, registration, and gasoline. So whether you are making car payments or not, this account will require regular deposits and withdrawals and careful record-keeping to keep you on the road.

When setting up your budget, it's always best to be conservative in your estimate. Set aside money each month to cover more than gas. Eventually, your car will need new tires, a new battery, a tune-up, or a major repair, and if you haven't been saving up money in this account, you'll be forced to cover these expenses with your savings.

If you're *really* smart, you'll also start setting aside money for your *next* car. The one you've just bought is eventually going to need to be replaced. If you tuck away money each month for that purpose, you'll have the cash to buy a better car next time around, *and* you'll have the value of your old car when you sell it. If you get into this habit, you'll never have to have a car loan.

Before You Buy

1. Go to the library and look through consumer information on cars. You'll find guides listing every car make, model, year, and the results of surveys taken by their owners.

   Through careful research you can learn about:

   a. The best buys.
   b. What features to look for in a car.
   c. How much you will have to save for the one you want.

2. Also,

   d. Interview car owners you know and perhaps talk to experts at car shows or car clubs.
   e. Make a list of the best dealership for used cars. Be sure they are reputable businesses that have been around for a while. You can phone the Better Business Bureau in your area to find out the business history of any establishment.

Rewind

1. New cars plunge in value the moment you drive them off the lot.

2. Avoid a car loan; pay cash for a reliable used car.

3. Read consumer guides to find the most reliable makes and models.

4. Read car ads for weeks to get a feel for prices.

5. Check out as many cars as you can before making a decision.

6. Ask the owner lots of questions to learn as much as you can about a car.

7. Give the car a thorough examination before you make a deal.

CHAPTER 14

How To Pay for College

OKAY, SO MY GRADE POINT AVERAGE ISN'T THAT GREAT, BUT MY RÉSUMÉ SAYS I'M ENTHUSIASTIC, A GOOD WORKER, WILLING TO LEARN AND I **LOVE** NEW CHALLENGES!

RECRUITER

Chapter 14

How To Pay for College

College has gotten pretty expensive these days. Many students and their families run up major debts to pay for it. But it's still possible to get a good education without going into financial bondage. This chapter tells you how.

If you're planning to attend college, you're about to face one of the biggest financial challenges of your life. Because the cost of higher education has increased so drastically during the last few years, most students and their families can't afford to pay for college without financial help. College financial assistance comes in three forms: scholarships, grants, and student loans. Let's look at each of these sources of money.

Scholarships

As you know, merit-based scholarships are awarded to students with high academic performance, artistic talent, or athletic ability. Some scholarships are *provisional*: If you fail to live up to the requirements, you must repay them. For example, some medical school scholarships come with the provision that you must practice in a rural area after graduation. If you fail to live up to your end of the bargain, you may get stuck with a repayment obligation three times the amount of the scholarship.

Some college scholarships come from

Scholarship Tips

When searching for available scholarships, keep these tips in mind.

- Ask a lot of questions; challenge promises.
- Get everything in writing.
- Weigh the odds before writing innumerable essays.
- Avoid college-fund gimmicks from insurance companies.
- Avoid scholarship search firms.

private foundations and organizations: chambers of commerce, service groups, church denominations, foundations, corporations, civic clubs, alumni associations, professional associations, and trade unions. Ask your high school guidance counselor, teachers, pastor, and other community leaders about what's available. Most high schools and colleges now have computer access to lists of financial aid sources, including scholarships.

Colleges and universities often have their own scholarships, which they use to recruit and reward superior students. Athletic scholarships get lots of attention in the press, but schools recruit academic talent too. Check with the college financial aid office for information and applications for these scholarships.

Grants

Federal and state grants for college education are available to students who have a great financial need. Like most scholarships, grant funds do not need to be repaid when you graduate. One such program is called the Pell Grant, which is available directly from the federal government to qualified undergraduates who can show a financial need. Another federal program is the Supplemental Educational Opportunity Grant, which is administered by the school.

The College Work-Study program (CWS) is a grant you work for. The college teams up with the federal or state government to provide money for your education. In turn, the college sets you up with an on-campus or off-campus job, sometimes in your field of study. Instead of paying you with a paycheck, the school pays you with an education.

Loans

In the 1980s the federal government responded to the rising costs of higher education by making it easier for students and their families to qualify and repay loans. They did this by offering low-interest loans of their own and offering to guarantee the loans of other institutions who lend to students.

The good news is that many more students can now afford to get a diploma. The bad news is that most of those students will be in financial bondage for years after graduation while they try to pay off their loans.

Federally guaranteed loans essentially make Uncle Sam the cosigner on a loan made by a bank or other financial institution. If *you* don't pay it back, *we* (the taxpayers of the United States) have to pay back the lender. Of course, the lender will still hound you to repay the loan so they can lend this money to the next student. And don't forget that your payments—or lack of them—leave a lasting mark on your young credit report.

With all of these loans available, it's tempting just to pay for your education with borrowed money and worry about the repayment later. To keep enrollments up, colleges have streamlined the complicated financial aid process, making it relatively simple for you to sign away a huge chunk of your future income. They want you in school, paying tuition, paying their bills, keeping the school in business.

Where the tuition money comes from is not a big concern to them, as long as it's paid. So *you* must be the one who guards your future. *You* must be sure that the financial aid help they're offering is best for you in the long run.

It's not easy to avoid the temptation of low-interest loans. Most people figure they'll be making lots of money after they graduate, and the monthly loan payments won't amount to much. And most of those folks learn that they figured wrong.

An annual salary of $20,000, $30,000, or $40,000 seems like a lot of cash when you've been working minimum wage jobs til now. But chances are, you've been living on a subsidy called *parents,* who pay the rent, fill the refrigerator, finance your braces, and keep you in clothes. But that subsidy soon ends, and all those bills will take a colossal chunk out of that seemingly large salary. When you stick a loan payment on top of it all, there may be nothing left. You'll find yourself longing for those subsidized days of minimum wage. We know of brilliant, hard–working adults in their thirties who are *still* paying off their college loans. There's got to be a better way.

There is. It's still possible to graduate from a good college, with a good education, without a heavy debt to haunt you. Here are some ideas.

Alternative Funding Ideas

The most economical plan is one of the most popular: Live at home, attend an inexpensive community college for one or two years, and work part-time to save up

money until you transfer to a four-year school. This may seem unappealing or unimpressive to some students. But four years later, those who carefully follow this plan graduate with the same diploma as their peers. And they do so with a lot less debt to tie them down after graduation.

Some students join the co-op program in their second year of college. This normally adds only one year to the total time it takes to earn a bachelor's degree, but it also adds approximately $8,000 a year in student income. Most universities have special departments that will give you the details. In essence, it means going to school one quarter, working the next. This program can provide valuable on-the-job experience, and it looks great on a resume when you're ready to hunt for a job after college.

The military offers money-earning opportunities for college students. If you join a reserve unit in the Army, Navy, Air Force, Marines, or Coast Guard, or enlist in the Air or Army National Guard, you'll be paid over $100 a month to attend a weekend drill; plus they'll drop another $190 in your lap every month you remain in school. And you pick up extra cash for training in the summer. And if you join the ROTC program as a junior, you'll get another $100 each month and return to your reserve unit as an officer when you graduate.

The Financial Aid Process

The federal government, your state government, and your college offer many forms of financial aid. The eligibility and application process for each of these sources varies. The best thing to do is to pick up a packet of financial aid information at the school you wish to attend. This packet contains information, worksheets, applications and a list of all the deadlines you'll need to know.

To make the complicated financial aid process easier, you can apply for most grants and loans using the same application form, called the Free Application for Federal Student Aid (FAFSA). It's available at the school's financial aid office. The FAFSA asks all sorts of questions about you and your family's finances; the government uses this information to determine which grants and loans you are eligible for.

Basically, the government uses the numbers you put down on your FAFSA to come up with a figure called the EFC, or Expected Family Contribution. This is the amount of money they figure you and your folks can afford to contribute to your education. If the EFC is less than the cost of tuition, books, and living expenses, the government and your school then point you to grants and loans that make up the difference.

Let's say that your family has an EFC of $4,000 and your school says that the cost of attending is $3,800 a year. You have no need for financial aid. That's great news! You can afford to attend school debt-free. If the cost of your education is $9,000 a year, then you'll be eligible for $5,000 a year in grants and low-interest loans.

As we said, the government uses your family's tax forms and other information you provide on the FAFSA to figure out your EFC. Some students and their families are tempted to fudge the numbers on these forms to make themselves eligible for grants and low-interest loans. But "fudging" is just a polite word for cheating, and "government" is merely a fancy word for *us*. In other words, the taxpayers are the ones being cheated. Honest, hardworking taxpayers fund those grants and subsidize the interest on these loans. *Somebody* has to work to pay for your education. Do your very best to pay for it yourself. And if that's not enough, *then* let the rest of us help you.

Your FAFSA must be submitted no earlier than January 1 of the calendar year you plan to start school. That's because it asks questions about your family's previous tax year, which won't be over until then. Some states have financial aid programs that require your completion of this form as early as March 1, so you should submit it as soon after January 1 as possible. It's a good incentive to get your parents to do their taxes early.

The financial aid process is complicated. It's essential that you get all the information you need, as soon as you can. Read *everything*; it will be good practice for college! No one expects you to become an expert in all the written information, so ask questions if something isn't clear. Your high school guidance counselor and the school's financial aid office staff are paid to help you.

Mark all deadlines in your calendar so you don't miss important application dates. And make sure you fill out every application accurately; the offices that process them have hundreds or thousands to shuffle, and they routinely send back anything that's not done right.

Finding a way to pay for college is complicated, but it's not impossible. Remember, with diligent effort and prayer, there *is* a way.

Rewind

1. Facing college is one of the biggest financial challenges of your life.

2. Scholarships are awarded to students with high academic performance, artistic talent, or athletic ability.

3. Colleges and universities have their own scholarships, which they use to recruit and reward superior students.

4. Federal and state grants for college education are available to students who have a great financial need.

5. The federal government responded to the rising costs of higher education by making it easier to qualify for and repay loans.

6. Most students will be in financial bondage for years after graduation while they try to pay off their loans.

7. Alternative funding can help you avoid heavy debt.

8. The military offers money-earning opportunities for college students.

CHAPTER 15

How To Get a Job

Chapter 15
How To Get a Job

Over half of all 16- to 19-year-olds work. Some love their jobs, others hate them. We'll show you how to land a job you like.

If you decide to join the teenage work force, you'll be getting much more than a paycheck for your efforts. A good job can give you great rewards. First, it shapes the way you perceive work. A good experience now will make work in the future better. Since you'll probably be working for the next 40 to 50 years of your life, it's nice to start off with a healthy perception.

A good job can also do wonders for your self-image. It's a good feeling to know that your boss and coworkers are depending on you to do a job that you know you can do. What's more, It exposes you to new people—good and bad. You may find yourself getting along great with people you never would have chosen as friends. Suddenly all your ideas about who's cool and who isn't don't apply.

Jobs Gone Bad

Teenage jobs can be great. But before you take one, you better look at the negative aspect: If you work too much during the school year, your education might suffer. Working late on school nights is the best way to sleep through your first two classes. You may lose valuable time for friends, sports, church, music, or some other important part of your life.

Working long hours at an unchallenging job can do more than use up your time and energy; it can make you cynical about work in general. The job becomes a necessary evil that you're willing to tolerate until you can afford to quit.

Unfortunately, many of the jobs open to you are just that: don't think, just push these little buttons, take the money, give back the change shown on the computer screen, and say "Have a nice day."

Some of your friends are working in jobs that pay well, but they are paying more in damage to their education, family, friendships, and self image than the fattest paycheck can compensate for. So before you start hunting for a job, you've got some work to do.

- Consider how many hours you can afford to work without doing damage to your other priorities. (What's your bottom line?)

- Interview friends who have jobs. Find out what they're learning and what negative effects the jobs have on their lives.

- Look at who you are and how that will affect the kind of job you might like: introvert, extrovert; organized, spontaneous; team player, lone ranger; earlybird, nightowl; frantic, methodical. A job that doesn't compliment your personality can make you miserable.

- Talk to your parents. You can work for the next 50 years if you want to, but you can never buy back the time you'll lose with your family.

If you determine that a job isn't right for you at the moment, that's great! If you believe that a job would be a positive addition to your life, that's great too. But the decision has to be yours.

Writing a Résumé

Before you hunt for the job of your dreams, you should put together a résumé, which is a summary of your most important work and educational accomplishments. At this point in your career you may be asking, "But what if I don't have any?" You do. One reason why you should write a resume before going out to look for a job is to show *yourself* how accomplished you are.

The first résumé you should write is intended for your eyes only: don't plan on handing it out to potential employers. Its purpose is to convince you that you've had valuable experiences which will help you do any job better. Résumés work even if you've had little or no formal job experience.

There are books available that will guide you in writing your résumé. If you don't have any of those, you might want to use the following suggestions.

1. List Your Job Experiences.

List all volunteer or paid jobs you've had, no matter how small or insignificant they may seem. Under each job, identify the main responsibilities and accomplishments.

- *Newspaper delivery*– delivered papers every day, solicited new subscribers, got few complaints, trained my replacement

- *Babysitting*– babysat for eight different families on regular basis; was considered reliable by parents and well liked by kids

- *Concession Stand Sales*– worked snack trailer at Little League a few times: sold food, worked cash register, cooked on the grill, learned how to set up the soda fountain

- *School Newspaper Reporter*– reporter for junior high newspaper: wrote one article per month, interviewed principal, teachers, and students; learned editing, layout, printing

2. Identify Your Strengths

These jobs won't astound any potential employer, but they should convince you that you have *strengths* that make you very hireable.

- work well under pressure (Little League concession stands are mob scenes after a game)
- reliable (the paper route and babysitting show you)
- trustworthy (most parents won't trust the lives of their kids with losers)
- know how to work within a deadline (reporter, newspaper delivery)
- teachable (learning new skills at the concession stand and school paper)
- can teach others (training your replacement with the newspaper route)
- have sales experience (concession stand and newspaper route)
- work well with adults (all your jobs)

3. Measure Your Accomplishments

What's lacking in the above list is any measure of how well you did. So go back through it and try to determine as many accomplishments as possible.

- As a newspaper deliverer you increased your route size 20 percent in three months by selling new subscriptions; you were awarded on three occasions for zero-complaint months. (No need to mention that in another month you hit someone's cat and broke a window).

- As a babysitter, you averaged five requests a week and babysat for one family over 50 times.

- At the concession stand you personally served up to 50 customers in one hour (and killed 12 cockroaches).

- And at the school newspaper you figured out a way to cut the printing and collating time in half.

4. Put It All Together

You are beginning to look like *Superworker*. Now rewrite your résumé, organizing it by job strengths (e.g., trustworthy, teachable, sales experience). Under each of these headings, list the specific accomplishments, using as many numbers as you can. After reading your finished résumé a few times, you should be convinced that you have great strengths and important job skills. And if you are convinced, you stand a good chance of convincing a potential employer.

If you are applying for a retail sales clerk position and the manager asks you if you've ever worked in a store before, you can reply, "No, but I've had some sales experience. I have worked at a baseball concession stand, handling as many as 50 customers in an hour; and I've sold newspaper subscriptions, increasing my paper route by 20 percent in three months. I know how to make customers smile, and I'm pretty good at knowing what to do when they're not happy." That sounds more impressive than saying that you sold hot dogs at a baseball game and got people to subscribe to the newspaper.

Job Hunting

Armed with a résumé, a clear idea of what you want from a job, and what skills you can bring to it, you're ready to look for a job. The following job-hunting techniques have proved to be successful.

Connections: If employers have a choice, they will hire people they know (or at least people

---

Résumé Writing Tips

- If you don't have lots of formal job experience, list your *skills* and *accomplishments* first.

- If you've had formal work experience, list your *jobs* first. Include the employer's name, the period you worked, your title, main job responsibilities, and any numbers that go with them. Start with the most recent job and work back in time.

- Make it neat! Appearance, grammar, and spelling speak volumes about who you are.

who know someone they know) before hiring complete strangers. That means the best way to look for a job is not in the want ads; it is among your family and friends. Ask your parents if they have any friends who own businesses or can somehow help you find a job where they work. Ask your own friends about open positions at their jobs. If your friends are good workers, their recommendations are worth a lot.

Trading Places: If you have a friend who is getting ready to quit a good job, you may be able to take his or her place. You will still have to sell yourself to the boss, but you've already got one foot in the door.

Pound the Pavement: Sometimes the best way to get a job is by going straight to the manager. Make a list of several potential employers; then stop by to apply. Ask for the manager, introduce yourself, and announce that you'd like to apply for a job. (Hint: If you're applying a restaurant, don't go in during the lunch or dinner rush.) Pick up an application and fill it out; or, better yet, take it home so you can fill it out more neatly. Then bring it back, stapled with your résumé. This gives you one more opportunity to see the manager, which may be twice as much as anyone else applying for the job.

New Business: Opening a new business is a major undertaking, and hiring employees is just one of many big steps. If you see a new business going in at a shopping center, see if you can get the owner's name from the center's management office. Call and tell the owner that you'd like to work in the new store and that you are available now. If the owner agrees to hire you, it's one less person he or she needs to worry about the week before the grand opening when things get really crazy and time is short. And you may be able to start early by helping to set up the store.

Source Search: You already know about the newspaper want ads. But there are other job listings available to you.

- The Chamber of Commerce may list summer job opportunities in your area.
- The Labor Department's U.S. Employment Service has offices in many cities throughout the country that list jobs in the area. You can find their number in the government section of the phone book.
- If you haven't already done so, check the job listings in your school's career center.
- Many churches and other community organizations sponsor job boards that list part-time and summer jobs open to teens. Get out the phone book and call as many of these organizations as you can locate. Even if they don't have a job board, they may be planning to fill a job for which you qualify.

The Winning Job Interview

Advertising agencies know that if their ad doesn't grab attention in that first second or so, the reader won't bother to read any further. An ad that fails in the first second is a failure—regardless of how good the rest of the ad is or the quality of the product it sells.

Now imagine that you and everyone else looking for a job are just advertisements in a magazine. The employer is flipping through the magazine very fast, deciding every moment whether to read an ad or turn the page.

Fortunately, if you have managed to meet the boss face to face, you have more than a few seconds to make your impression: you have an entire minute! In that first minute of an introduction or an interview, your potential employer is going to make some important decisions about you. There are ways to make every second count.

Dress: Wear what you would wear on the job if you were hired. If you're unsure, it's better to be overdressed than underdressed, but be sure you feel comfortable. If you feel strange, you look strange.

Grooming: Look as neat and well-groomed as you can. You don't want the person interviewing you to be thinking about how you look while you are trying to impress him or her with who you are and what you can do.

Body Language: Offer to shake hands when you meet; age and gender don't matter. Give a firm, friendly grip. (Translation: "Meeting you is important to me.") Look directly at the person's face when you speak. ("I believe in what I'm saying.") Do the same when you're listening to people. ("I care about what you are saying.")

Conversation: Your ability to communicate is being evaluated. When meeting, state your name clearly. If the person has forgotten your name, save him or her the embarrassment of having to ask. Address an interviewer by his or her last name until you're given permission to use the first name. Use the name frequently; people like to hear their names.

Other Interview Tips

Find out as much as you can about the business before you go in for an interview. If it's a big company, it probably is listed in one of the corporate directories at the public library. Ask the librarian where to look. You also can call friends who've worked there. The more you know, the more intelligent you'll sound during your interview. It also will be obvious to your prospective employer that you care enough to do some homework.

Write a list of questions you have about the job responsibilities and expectations and the company in general. The answers will help you decide if the job is right for you.

Write questions you likely will be asked. Have a friend or family member interview you using these questions so you can get comfortable talking about yourself. This also will teach you how to be more concise when you answer.

Bad Interviews

Some of the reasons employers give for not hiring student workers:

- poor personal appearance
- overbearing, know-it-all
- inability to express self clearly, poor diction and grammar
- lack of interest, enthusiasm
- interested only in paycheck
- wants too much too soon
- makes excuses, is evasive
- lack of tact
- lack of courtesy
- lack of vitality
- little sense of humor
- lazy

The following are some common job interview questions, as well as some tips to help you answer them.

Question	Answer
Tell me about yourself.	Make it short and sweet: your school, grade, family, interests.
What subjects do you enjoy? Why?	Be honest, show enthusiasm over things you like.
Sports? Hobbies? Other interests?	Again, show enthusiasm and a sense of dedication for the things you care about.
Do you drive? Own a car?	The real question: "Can you be counted on to get here on time?" and "Can you run errands that require driving?" If you don't have a car, assure the interviewer that you have a reliable means of getting to work.
What are your strengths?	What the interviewer wants to hear: "I work hard, learn fast, and I'm reliable." If it's true, say it.
What are your weaknesses?	"Acceptable" weaknesses are when you have too much of a good thing: perfectionist, too task-oriented, overly self-critical.
What are your future plans?	Anything ambitious sounds better than "I don't really know."
What days and hours can you work?	Have a copy of your schedule; be honest about non-negotiables: school, study, church, family time.
Why do you want to work here?	Good place to work, challenging, nice co-workers, good reputation, quality product—whatever is true.

After the Interview

Send a thank you letter to the person who interviewed you. If there was more than one interviewer, write the note to the one who has the power to hire you. Mail the letter that day so the person doesn't have an opportunity to forget you. Now continue your job search: meet managers, line up interviews. In other words, keep working at it. Your goal is to have at least two or three offers from which to choose.

When you get a job offer, generally by phone, thank the person sincerely. Make a note of the details: starting date, wage, hours, and so on. Tell the employer that you'd like to accept, but you need a day to discuss it with your family. Talk it over with your parents and some close friends. Compare the job offer to your original goals, because sometimes in the excitement of landing a job you can lose sight of your own best interests.

Also, if you applied anywhere else for a position that you'd like to have more than the one you've been offered, call that employer. Explain that you got another job offer, but explain that you would rather work for him or her. If that employer says no, you can accept the first offer. But if you are offered a better job (where you'd rather work), then you're set. You have a job either way, and you can be confident that you got the best opportunity available.

Write a Résumé

Use the format in this chapter. You also can find résumé examples in books and computer programs.

Job Experiences:

    1. _____

    2. _____

    3. _____

    4. _____

    5. _____

Strengths:

    1. _____

    2. _____

    3. _____

    4. _____

    5. _____

Accomplishments:

    1. _____

    2. _____

    3. _____

    4. _____

    5. _____

Put it together using the form on page 140.

Rewind

1. A job can provide you with income, experience, and new friendships. But it can also steal time from other priorities in your life. As a student, you must weigh the advantages with the disadvantages to decide if working is best for you.

2. A résumé helps convince *you* that you have hirable skills. It also can show a prospective employer what these skills are.

3. Want ads and job boards are just two ways to find a job. Other methods include asking friends and going door to door.

4. When meeting a prospective employer, you have just a few minutes to convince that person that you are worthy of the job: make every effort to present yourself well—in appearance, actions, and language.

5. Every job interview, good or bad, is a lesson in selling yourself. Learn from your mistakes and turn them into strengths for the next interview.

notes

_____

_____

_____

_____

_____

_____

_____

_____

_____

_____

_____

_____

CHAPTER

16

How To Keep a Job

Chapter 16
How To Keep a Job

Getting hired has a lot to do with first impressions. Staying hired means making a lasting impression. Here are some ideas to help you keep the job you get, and keep yourself healthy and growing in the process.

Most of us have a tough time making it through the first days or weeks of a new job. Everything and everyone is new to us, and it's easy to make mistakes. Employers understand that your first days may be rough, and generally they'll cut you some slack. But there comes a time when you had better do your job right. If you want to keep it, you'll have to deliver. Here's how.

Learn Everything You Can

Most teenagers think the reason why they're working is for the money. But if you're not learning everything you can while on that job, you're making a poor investment of your time and energy.

Training new workers is an expensive and tiring task for managers. Sometimes they'd rather keep a mediocre employee than to have to go through the hassle of hiring and training a new one.

Knowledge is job insurance. The more you know, the more difficult you are to replace.

On-the-job learning pays dividends in other ways. It keeps you from getting bored when things are slow. You can teach others what you know; and, if you're good at it, you're in the best position to get a promotion. Also, what you learn may help in future jobs. It might even help you to successfully launch your own business.

Make a list of tasks other people are doing where you work, from loading receipt paper into the cash register to filling out reports to reordering merchandise from a supplier. If you have finished your responsibilities, choose something off the list and ask someone to teach you. Think of it this way: unlike school, you're actually *getting paid to learn*. Grasp every opportunity to do so.

Do What's Right

Your job is one of the toughest proving grounds for your integrity. Behavior that was not approved of at home or among your friends may be standard conduct at the workplace. Sometimes people who disapprove of lying, cheating, and stealing have no problem calling in sick when they aren't, stretching the hours on their time card, or taking home supposedly free merchandise (pens, pencils, tape, or any assortment of supplies). If you want to keep your job, be completely honest and above reproach.

Behave according to what you know is right, not according to the code of ethics that you see other workers following.

That's not an easy thing to do. In lots of jobs, it seems impossible not to cheat. The problem with cheating is that it's so habit-forming. Some people find it thrilling to rearrange things to suit their desires. They figure they are getting something for nothing and that's great because they can remember so many times when they got *nothing* after working harder than anyone. But these people usually find that if they cheat enough, trying to cope with life as it really is (without changing to suit them) becomes a real drag. And it doesn't take long: cheating is a strong drug, and it can be addictive.

It's true: sometimes cheaters do prosper. But honest people attain their goals without sacrificing character or integrity. At some point in their lives, most people stop being consumed by where they're going and pay more attention to how they're getting there.

The Bible has many verses that warn against cheating (deception). One says, [The one] *who walks in a blameless way is the one who will minister to me.* [The one] *who practices deceit* [cheating] *shall not dwell within my house;* [the one] *who speaks falsehood shall not maintain his* [or her] *position before me"* (Psalm 101:6–7).

Give the Boss a Break

Most bosses are easy to please. In many businesses, employers have put up with so many irresponsible workers that one who simply shows up on time makes "employee of the month." Most employers would list the following five traits in a description of the ideal employee.

1. *Punctual:* Showing up late, leaving early, and failing to come at all are among an employer's biggest headaches. When you're supposed to be there but aren't, either work isn't being done or people more responsible than you are taking up the slack. If you think changing your habits to get to work on time is tough now, wait until you are 25 or 30 and that habit is as much a part of you as your name. It's now or never.

   Show up five minutes early every day. If you have a perfect attendance record for the week, treat yourself to a frozen yogurt or something else you'd consider a reward. Do not call in sick unless you are sick. Nobody likes being lied to. If you've agreed to work that day, do it. If you'd like a day off, plan ahead. Get someone to work for you. Above all, shoot straight with your boss. It's important that your employer is able to trust you.

2. *Cooperative:* Almost every job is a team effort. It doesn't matter how well you work if you can't get along with others. Sometimes being a boss is like being the referee of a professional wrestling match: employees gossiping, backbiting, fighting, and occasionally getting into a skirmish. Play fair, do your best to get along with others, and follow directions. You'll be an asset.

3. *Assertive:* "Just do it": Nike's famous slogan applies in your job. Until you do, you're just a machine. When you are told to do something, you do it. Initiative is a human trait: You decide that you will do something, and you do it. Make a list of the things your boss tells you to do. The next day, do them all before he has a chance to tell you.

4. *Enthusiastic:* On the job there's one thing worse than being unhappy: being the boss of someone who's unhappy. If you have any reason to be excited about your job, let it show. Enthusiasm is contagious. The goal is to spread that enthusiasm around.

5. *Honest:* Lying about the number of hours you worked, giving out freebies to your friends, helping yourself to merchandise without permission—it seems like "everybody's doin' it." No, not everyone. There actually are some honest people left who will refuse to lie, cheat, or steal. Join them.

6. *Fun:* It's okay to have fun at work. There are very few jobs where it's inappropriate to laugh, smile, or joke with customers and coworkers. If you are getting your job done and not destroying things or offending people, you're probably making your workplace more pleasant for workers and customers. With a little creativity, you can turn even a boring job into a fun experience.

The above qualities are actually a pretty good guide for all of us regarding Christian behavior. The apostle Paul gave a similar list in his letter to Christians living in the in the city of Philippi: *"Finally, brethren, whatever is true, whatever is honorable, whatever is right, whatever is pure, whatever is lovely, whatever is of good repute, if there is any excellence and if anything worthy of praise, let your mind dwell on these things"* (Philippians 4:8).

Like your first love, your first job leaves an indelible impression on you. It will affect the way you see work for the rest of your life. Do everything in your power to make your job the best experience possible.

Top Employee Tips

If you have a job or will be getting one, think about what you could do to be a better employee. Make a list of things you could do at the job site that would make your employer feel really good about you working there.

1. _____
2. _____
3. _____
4. _____
5. _____
6. _____

If there are possibilities for promotions, make a list of qualities your employer may be looking for in that next level.

1. _____
2. _____
3. _____
4. _____
5. _____
6. _____

Maybe even ask your employer what he or she is looking for in the next candidate for promotion. Try to work on those qualities.

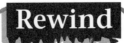

1. A job is like an education you get paid to receive. Learn everything you can.

2. A job is proving ground for your integrity. Do what you know is right, not what others claim is okay.

3. Make your boss's tough job easier by being punctual, cooperative, assertive, enthusiastic, honest, and fun.

4. Make your first job experience the best you can. The impressions you take with you will last the rest of your life.

notes

CHAPTER 17

How To Rock the World with Your Money

Chapter 17

How To Rock the World with Your Money

Lots of teenagers say that they're not old enough, smart enough, rich enough, or "whatever" enough, to change the world. So they sit around and wait for that magical age when God can finally use them to make a difference. Guess what? God doesn't check for I.D.s at the Kingdom door. He can use you right now to effect a change in your community and culture. Get out your money. . . and look out world!

Vote with Your Money

Every dollar you spend on something is a vote for the values that product conveys. Every time you pay $7 to watch a violent film, you are saying to Hollywood: "Violence sells; make more violent films."

When you buy a CD or cassette that celebrates the Christian faith, you are telling the musicians and the manufacturer to make more. Every purchase is a vote. When you buy *good* products, you are casting your vote for more good products.

Lots of folks complain about the trash they see in movies, music, television, video games, books, and magazines. Then they "vote" *for* these things with their dollars. Most of the people who produce these things aren't dead set on making the world a trashier place. They're just trying to make money. If they could make more money producing good merchandise, they'd make more. And those who are already producing good products would make a lot more.

You might be saying, "I'm just one vote. They won't notice what *I* do." You are right, of course. Your purchase alone isn't going to make or break any business. However, it still counts. When your friends decide to go to a trashy movie, you could politely excuse yourself. When they ask why, tell them. Yes, some may laugh at you; and they'll probably go without you, but maybe your best friend will respect your choice and won't go either. That's two votes!

And, if you can convince your other friends to see a better movie, maybe that's three or four votes. When you do this several times, with enough friends, and enough of *their* friends, people start to talk. Then it becomes an *issue*.

If enough people go to good movies instead of bad ones, the theater notices. They're just trying to make money. And if good movies sell, they'll show more good movies. Now you've got a *movement*.

Then again maybe not. Your "dollar votes" may have little or no effect on the producers of the world's products. But, the fact remains: when you pay for bad things, you are contributing to what's bad. And that feels wrong. When you pay for good things, you're contributing to what's good. And that feels right.

There's another reason to vote with your money. You are managing God's money for Him, and He does care what you do with it. Use His money well—for *good* things.

Shop Locally

Some people are funny: They'll drive around a parking lot for ten minutes, just to get the closest parking space, risking life and limb as they race and weave through traffic, just to get home one minute faster. They'll burn $2 worth of gasoline to drive across town so they can save a few cents at a cheaper gas station. But *first, fastest, cheapest* isn't always *best*.

This is especially true with money. Let's say that you're shopping for shoes. You've got your heart set on a new pair of state-of-the-art sneakers: they've got hydro-electric soles, titanium-alloy heel supports, and remote-control laces. Your neighborhood shoe store sells them for $65. The big discount store in the next town sells them for $55. Why waste $10? So you hop in the car; drive an hour, round-trip; and get the ultimate shoes for the ultimate price.

If price were everything, you would have made the right move. But look at the big picture.

First, you spent $4 in gas. Okay, so you saved $6 (the $10 saving on price minus $4 for gas). But while you were at the discount store, where they sell everything you could ever want, you spotted a "great price" on music CDs, so you bought one for $10. Now you've actually spent *more* money because you had no intention of buying that CD (and you'll be tired of listening to it soon anyway).

There are other "prices" too. There's the extra air pollution from driving all those miles. There's also a community price, because the owner of your local shoe store lives in your town, employs your neighbors, sends his kids to your school, and pays taxes that pay for your police, fire department, street repair, and the upkeep of that park where you and your friends go.

COUNTING ALL THE COSTS

DISCOUNT-O-RAMA	
shoes	$ 55
gas to drive there	4
impulse CD purchase	10
air pollution	?
income lost to local citizens	65
taxes lost to community	?
Total cost:	$69
(plus impact on family, environment, community, and taxes)	

DIPPY'S SHOE STORE	
shoes	$65
(walk to store)	0
(no CDs at Dippy's)	0
(clean air)	
(no loss to local workers)	0
(no loss to local taxes)	0
Total cost	$65

When you spend your money locally, you invest in your community. And when you *vote with your money* in your community, you have a powerful effect on lives.

Does this mean it's wrong to shop outside your community? Of course not. But it *does* mean that, as God's manager, you must look at *all* the price tags: financial, social, spiritual. Make every one of God's dollars do the most *good*—for his glory.

Invest Locally

There's another way to make sure that your money makes a difference in your community. Deposit it in a local bank. It's easy to understand why a neighborhood store is an important part of the community. People have to eat. But why is a local bank important?

It goes like this: The bank uses the money in your savings account to make loans to people and businesses in your community. Let's say that the bank took your savings, combined it with lots of other accounts, and lent it to a woman to help her open a sporting goods store. She used the money to pay a carpenter to renovate the building.

The carpenter used some of the money to buy lumber. The lumberyard owner used some of *that* money to hire a new manager. The manager used some of his new salary to pay the property taxes on his house. The schools used some of the property taxes to buy computers for their classrooms.

The students who use these computers will become more successful. They'll earn more money, deposit more of it at the bank, and the bank will lend more money to other businesses . . . and so on.

And we didn't even mention the employees that were hired at the new sporting goods store, and where they spent *their* paychecks. Nor did we mention how much money some of these people gave back to God, and voted with *their* dollars, and . . . you get the picture.

When possible, *invest* in your community.

Give, Give, Give

We talked about this at length in another chapter. Giving is the most powerful way to change the world with your dollars. God always manages to do better things with the money you give than you could do with it.

The world is filled to the brim with great needs. And governments can argue till the end of time about how to solve these problems. But you can do something *now*.

Every time you give you become a world changer. You're part of the solution. And God applauds your efforts because you're showing that your priorities are His priorities. *You* can help to change the world with *your* money.

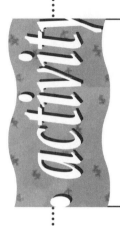

Research and Review

1. Think about a movie, book, or product that you have seen or purchased recently and have strong feelings about.

2. Do some research to find out if your impressions are accurate.

3. If you feel others should know, write a review of the movie, book, or product for your church bulletin board or school paper.

Rewind

1. Every time you buy something, you're voting with your dollars. Buy *good* things, and the people who make them will make more.

2. Buying locally supports the people and services in your own community. And it gives you a bigger vote in what's best for your community.

3. Investing locally puts your money to work in the lives of your neighbors.

4. Regular giving makes you a part of the solution to the world's problems.

notes

Earnings Records

Week of: _____

Date	Income Source	Amount

Week of: _____

Date	Income Source	Amount

Week of: _____

Date	Income Source	Amount

Week of: _____

Date	Income Source	Amount

Creating Your Résumé

Fill in the information below.

NAME: _____
Address: _____
City/State/Zip: _____
Phone: _____

EDUCATION: _____
_____
_____
_____
_____
_____
_____
_____

EXPERIENCE: _____
_____
_____
_____
_____
_____
_____
_____
_____
_____
_____
_____

ACTIVITIES/
INTERESTS: _____
_____
_____
_____
_____
_____
_____

REFERENCES _____
_____
_____

Individual Account Sheets

ACCOUNT NAME

DATE	TRANSACTION	DEPOSIT	W/DRAW	BALANCE

Monthly Income & Expenses

Annual Income _____

Monthly Income _____

LESS

1. Charitable Giving _____

2. Tax _____

NET SPENDABLE INCOME _____

3. Housing (30%) _____

Mortgage (Rent) _____

Insurance _____

Taxes _____

Electricity _____

Gas _____

Water _____

Sanitation _____

Telephone _____

Maintenance _____

Other _____

4. Food (17%) _____

5. Auto(s) (15%) _____

Payments _____

Gas & Oil _____

Insurance _____

License _____

Taxes _____

Maint/Repair/
Replacement _____

6. Insurance (5%) _____

Life _____

Medical _____

Other _____

7. Debts (5%) _____

Credit Cards _____

Loans & Notes _____

Other _____

8. Enter. / Recreation (7%) _____

Eating Out _____

Trips _____

Babysitters _____

Activities _____

Vacation _____

Other _____

9. Clothing (5%) _____

10. Savings (5%) _____

11. Medical Expenses (5%) _____

Doctor _____

Dental _____

Drugs _____

Other _____

12. Miscellaneous (6%) _____

Toiletry, Cosmetics _____

Beauty, Barber _____

Laundry, Cleaning _____

Allowances, Lunches_____

Subscriptions, Gifts _____
(Incl. Christmas)

Special Education _____

Cash _____

Other _____

TOTAL EXPENSES _____

Net Spendable Income _____

Difference _____

Christian Financial Concepts

Teaching Biblical Principles of Managing Money

Larry Burkett, founder and president of Christian Financial Concepts, is the best-selling author of more than 50 books on business and personal finances. He also hosts two of CFC's four radio programs broadcast on hundreds of stations worldwide.

Larry earned B.S. degrees in marketing and in finance, and recently an Honorary Doctorate in Economics was conferred by Southwest Baptist University. For several years Larry served as manager in the space program at Cape Canaveral, Florida. He also has been vice president of an electronics manufacturing firm. Larry's education, business experience, and solid understanding of God's Word enable him to give practical, Bible-based financial counsel to families, churches, and businesses.

Founded in 1976, Christian Financial Concepts is a nonprofit, nondenominational ministry dedicated to helping God's people gain a clear understanding of how to manage their money according to scriptural principles. Although practical assistance is provided on many levels, the purpose of CFC is simply *to bring glory to God by freeing His people from financial bondage so they may serve Him to their utmost.*

One major avenue of ministry involves the training of volunteers in budget and debt counseling and linking them with financially troubled families and individuals through a nationwide referral network. CFC also provides financial management seminars and workshops for church and other groups. (Formats available include audio, video, and live instruction.) A full line of printed and audio-visual materials related to money management is available through CFC's materials department (1–800–722–1976) or via the Internet (http://www.cfcministry.org).

Life Pathways, another outreach of Christian Financial Concepts, helps teenagers and adults find their occupational calling. The Life Pathways *Career Direct* assessment package gauges a person's work priorities, skills, vocational interests, and personality. Reports in each of these areas define a person's strengths, weaknesses, and unique, God-given pattern for work.

Visit CFC's Internet site at http://www.cfcministry.org or write to the address below for further information.

Christian Financial Concepts
PO Box 2377
Gainesville, GA 30503

Money Matters for Kids and Teens™
Teaching Kids to Manage God's Gifts

Lauree and L. Allen Burkett are the founders of **Money Matters for Kids**™. God has planted in their hearts the commitment to see the next generation grounded in God's Word and living His principles. The vision of **Money Matters for Kids**™ is to provide children and teens with the tools they need to understand the Biblical principles of stewardship and to encourage them to live by those principles.

Visit our Web site at **www.mmforkids.org.** We welcome your comments and suggestions.

Money Matters for Kids
Lynden, Washington 98264–9760

Lightwave Publishing is a recognized leader in developing quality resources that encourage, assist, and equip parents to build Christian faith in their families.

Lightwave Publishing also has a fun kids' Web site and an internet-based newsletter called *Tips & Tools for Spiritual Parenting.* This newsletter helps parents with issues such as answering their children's questions, helping make church more exciting, teaching children how to pray, and much more.

For more information, visit Lightwave's Web site at **www.lightwavepublishing.com**

Moody Press, a ministry of Moody Bible Institute, is designed for education, evangelization, and edification.

If we may assist you in knowing more about Christ and the Christian life, please write us without obligation:

Moody Press, c/o MLM
Chicago, IL 60610

Or visit us at Moody's Web site: **www.moodypress.org**